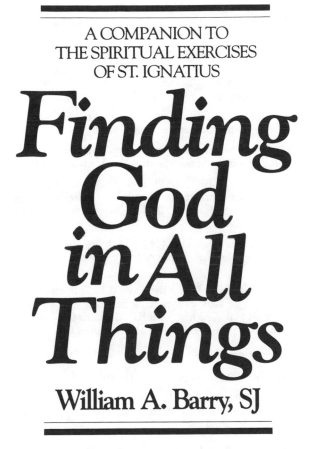

A COMPANION TO
THE SPIRITUAL EXERCISES
OF ST. IGNATIUS

Finding God in All Things

William A. Barry, SJ

AVE MARIA PRESS
Notre Dame, Indiana 46556

Imprimi Potest
Very Rev. Robert E. Manning, S.J., Provincial
Society of Jesus of New England

Scripture taken from the HOLY BIBLE, NEW INTERNATIONAL
VERSION. Copyright 1973, 1978, 1984 International Bible Society. Used
by permission of Zondervan Bible Publishers.

Portions of Chapter 2 first appeared in *Human Development*; portions of
Chapter 5 appeared in *America* and in *Soundings*, published by the Center
of Concern in Washington, D.C. Permission to use this material is
gratefully acknowledged.

Excerpts from *The Spiritual Exercises of St. Ignatius*, trans. Louis J. Puhl.
Copyright 1968 by Loyola University Press. Used by permission.

Excerpts taken from *Choosing Christ in the World*; published with the
permission of the Institute of Jesuit Sources, St. Louis, Missouri.

Excerpts from THE AUTOBIOGRAPHY OF St. IGNATIUS LOYOLA,
edited by John C. Olin, translated by Joseph F. O'Callaghan. Copyright ©
1974 by John C. Olin and Joseph F. O'Callaghan. Reprinted by permission
of HarperCollins Publishers.

Excerpts from TELLING THE TRUTH by Frederick Buechner. Copyright
© 1977 by Frederick Buechner. Reprinted by permission of HarperCollins
Publishers.

Excerpts from RETURN OF THE KING by J.R.R. Tolkien. Copyright ©
1955, 1965 by J.R.R. Tolkien. Copyright © renewed 1983 by Christopher
R. Tolkien, Michael H.R. Tolkien, John F.R. Tolkien, and Priscilla M.A.R.
Tolkien. Reprinted by permission of Houghton Mifflin Co.

International Standard Book Number: 0-87793-461-4
                                     0-87793-460-6 (Pbk.)

Library of Congress Catalog Card Number: 91-72115

Cover and text design by Elizabeth J. French
Cover photography by Justin A. Soleta

Printed and bound in the United States of America.

To all my brother Jesuits,
especially to those of the New England Province
and to Pedro Arrupe, S.J.,
who now prays for the Society he
led with such vision and love,
I dedicate this book with gratitude and hope and love
in this Ignatian Year 1990–1991

Contents

Acknowledgments

In the academic year 1988–89 the Jesuit Community and the University Chaplaincy at Boston College co-sponsored a series called "The University at Prayer," for which various members of the faculty and administration were invited to make presentations. The program continued in 1989–90. The committee appointed to propose programs for the year-long celebration of the Ignatian Year — from September 27, 1990, the 450th anniversary of the founding of the Society of Jesus, until July 31, 1991, the 500th year since the birth of Ignatius — suggested that I give all the presentations in "The University at Prayer" series for 1990–91 on themes of *The Spiritual Exercises*. This book is adapted from that series of talks. Ignatius' spiritual classic has inspired Jesuits and many others for over 450 years. I hope that *Finding God in All Things* will illuminate the spirituality of Ignatius and encourage those who have not yet experienced the transforming power of the Spiritual Exercises to try them.

I dedicate the book to my Jesuit brothers without whom I would not have experienced in my own life the transforming impact of the Spiritual Exercises. I believe that God led me into the companionship of the Society of Jesus over forty years ago for my good and happiness and for the "help of souls," as Ignatius puts it. I have had a very happy life and hope that I have been a help to others on the way to life.

I remember with special gratitude the late Pedro Arrupe, who led the Society with great courage, vision, and love during the challenging and difficult years after the Second Vatican Council. He gave me and many other Jesuits hope in dark hours because he exuded such confidence in God and in us and challenged us to come to grips with the modern world from the depths of the spirituality of the

5

Spiritual Exercises. This dedication is my small way of saying "thanks" to my brothers in the Lord, past, present, and future.

I want to thank J. Donald Monan, S.J., President of Boston College, and Joseph Duffy, S.J., Chair, and the Boston College committee for planning the university's celebration of the Ignatian Year, for their encouragement of this project, and for their confidence in me to pull it off. I am grateful to the sponsors of "The University at Prayer" series. There are no words to convey my profound gratitude to Ms. Kerry Maloney not only for the original inspiration for the series and the energy with which she organized the first two years, but especially for the warmth of her encouragement and enthusiasm for the present project. Moreover, she read all the first drafts as soon as I had them ready and gave me enthusiastic feedback as well as very helpful suggestions. I do not believe that I could have done it without her.

I want to thank Marika Geoghegan, Mary Guy, O.S.U., Harvey Egan, S.J., Timothy Shannon, S.J., and Philomena Sheerin, M.M.M., who generously read the manuscript and gave me positive feedback and helpful suggestions. I am especially grateful to Harvey Egan for his attention to detail and for giving me the benefit of his great knowledge of Ignatian spirituality. His encouragement meant a great deal to me.

During the preparation of the talks and of this book I have been the rector of the Jesuit Community at Boston College. The fact that I had the energy to do this project says a great deal about my enjoyment not only of the community but of my job. Individual community members have also been very supportive of the project. Without the people who helped with the administrative work needed for a very large community of Jesuits I would not have been able to write this book. So I thank Lawrence Foley, S.J., Joseph

6

Killilea, Paul Nash, S.J., and Francis Venuta, S.J., who do so many things within and for the community that make our life together harmonious. I owe a special debt of gratitude to the community secretary, Cyrilla Mooradian, and to the administrator, James M. Collins, S.J.; without these two I would be lost.

Finally, since 1972, I have been privileged to direct hundreds of people through the Spiritual Exercises in retreats of various kinds and durations. Their great desires and openness and honesty with me have taught me much about how the Exercises foster a developing relationship with God, and I thank them all. Often during these retreats I have been privileged to work with teams of directors and to have profited from mutual supervision with them. I am grateful to all these co-workers, but especially to William J. Connolly, S.J., Robert G. Doherty, S.J., Anne Harvey, S.N.D., Paul Lucey, S.J., Joseph E. McCormick, S.J., and Francine Zeller, O.S.F., with whom I worked so closely in the early days of the individually directed Exercises and at the Center for Religious Development in Cambridge, Massachusetts.

Finally, I thank Frank Cunningham and Ken Peters of Ave Maria Press for their encouragement and suggestions.

Foreword

For over 450 years the Spiritual Exercises of St. Ignatius of Loyola have had a profound impact not only on many individuals but also on the world and the church. Originally people were directed individually through these exercises, but with the passage of time and a desire to expand their influence, group retreats of three or eight or thirty days became the norm. The Exercises were also adapted for parish missions and other forms of preached retreats. Only within recent years has individual direction become, once again, a preferred way to make the Spiritual Exercises. For those to whom the Spiritual Exercises are relatively unknown I want to give an overview that will serve as an outline of this book.

The book of *The Spiritual Exercises* is a compilation of notes mainly for the director of the Exercises. It contains a definition of the term "spiritual exercises," introductory annotations by Ignatius about the process and the attitudes of both the director and the one who makes the Exercises, a First Principle and Foundation, and then material for prayer divided into four "weeks."

The four "weeks," the heart of the process of "making the Exercises," are not to be construed as calendar weeks; rather, they refer to a variable period of time during which the retreatants experience a particular desire for God's intervention.

In the "First Week" the retreatants want God to reveal to them their sins and sinful tendencies so that they can repent of them and be converted. This desire presumes that retreatants trust God enough to have such a desire. Because many people need help to come to such trust in God, Chapter 1 begins with a discussion of how to let God heal life's hurts so that we can trust God. Once that trust is present, retreatants begin to desire to know how God sees them with all their sins and sinful tendencies. But retreatants vary in how much time they need in order to let God fulfill their desire. At bottom the desire is to know that God still loves us, warts and all.

In Chapter 2, I describe the experience that underlies the First Principle and Foundation. Chapter 3 describes the process of the "First Week." Because we are aware of living in a sinful world, I have included Chapter 4 on God's view of the world as part of the dynamic of this first "week."

In the "Second Week" retreatants who have realized how much Jesus loves them in spite of, or even because of, their sins desire to know Jesus better in order to love him more and to follow him more closely. This "week," again, varies in length depending on the retreatant and the retreatant's relationship with Jesus. Chapters 5 through 9 describe the process of this most important "week" in the Exercises.

Retreatants who come to know and love Jesus deeply as a friend and companion may also grow into the desire to share in the sufferings and agony of his passion and death. This desire ushers in the "Third Week" in which retreatants accompany Jesus on his final dark journey. When the desire to share Christ's passion and death has been fulfilled, then retreatants desire to share the joy of Jesus' resurrection which ushers in the "Fourth Week." Chapter 10 takes up the process of these two "weeks."

The final contemplation proposed to retreatants in the Spiritual Exercises is "The Contemplation to Obtain Divine Love," which is a recapitulation of the essence of Ignatian spirituality. In this contemplation retreatants desire to know in their bones how much God loves them so that they can return that love in some measure and also find God in all things. Chapter 11 describes that contemplation.

Ignatius thought that a properly prepared person with strong desires for God could go through this dynamic process in about thirty days. But he was also astute enough to know that people differ in their abilities, their desires, and their preparation. So he advised directors to adapt the exercises contained in his book to the individual. My own experience tells me that the full experience of the dynamic process of the Spiritual Exercises may take a lifetime. It is, however, a lifetime that is exciting, challenging, and eminently worth the effort.

What Are Spiritual Exercises?

I suspect that most people in the world and even in the Christian world have never heard of *The Spiritual Exercises* of Ignatius of Loyola, Jesuit megalomania notwithstanding. That does not bother me. What does concern me is the fact that many, if not most, people who have heard about the Spiritual Exercises think of them as something esoteric, something reserved for novices or vowed members of religious communities, for holy people, or at least for people who can get away to a retreat house for an extended period of time. Such an image has, unfortunately, kept a treasure from broad use in the church. This book will, I hope, dispel that image and invite readers to consider how they might use the Spiritual Exercises to benefit their relationship with God.

Inigo [Ignatius] of Loyola was a Basque warrior with a fiery temper and a romantic love of chivalry. Badly wounded in a battle with the French at the town of Pamplona, Inigo was taken back to his brother's castle of Loyola where he suffered two excruciating operations to set his shattered leg. He underwent the second operation so that he could still cut a dashing figure in the hosiery of the time. During his convalescence he engaged in two sets of vivid daydreams. In one set he dreamt of doing great deeds of chivalry and of

11

winning the favor of a great lady, probably a princess. These daydreams would last for hours and gave him great pleasure. He also began to dream of following Christ in great hardship and of imitating the saints after reading a life of Christ and a book of the lives of the saints. This second set of dreams also gave him great pleasure. One day he noticed that there was a difference in the experience of these different daydreams. When he finished the dreams of doing the great deeds of chivalry, he felt sad and out of sorts; but when he finished the dreams of following Christ and imitating the saints, he continued to feel joyous and content. He concluded that the dreams of following Christ were inspired by God, or, in his own terminology, the good spirit, and that the dreams of doing great knightly deeds were inspired by the bad spirit. This discernment of different spirits began his conversion.[1]

Inigo was twenty-six years old when he left his brother's castle on a donkey and journeyed to the little town of Manresa, not far from the Benedictine monastery of Montserrat. Here this theologically illiterate layman spent about eight months in intense prayer and ascetic practices. The months at Manresa transformed him from a somewhat self-centered, egotistical man bent on his own efforts to gain sanctity to a man who trusted that God was leading him toward an apostolic life of helping others to find God as he had done. During his own "spiritual exercises" he had begun to write down notes, and he continued to expand on these notes as he directed others through the various exercises. These notes eventually became the book *The Spiritual Exercises*.

As we noted in the Foreword, the book essentially consists of notes or directions for the director of the Exercises. In it one finds directions for helping people to make a general and particular examination of conscience and to engage in various forms of prayer ranging from vocal prayer and methods of saying vocal prayers to meditation and contemplation.

It contains rules for the discernment of spirits, rules for eating, rules for thinking with the church.

The Exercises proper are divided into four "weeks," each division referring to a dynamic that may take more or less than a week's time to happen. The first "week" is taken up with the dynamic of letting God reveal to the retreatant his or her sins and sinful tendencies in order that the retreatant might repent of them and realize that in spite of them he or she is a loved sinner. The second "week" is devoted to the following of Christ, getting to know him better in order to love him more and to follow him more closely. In the third "week" the retreatant desires to share with Jesus the sufferings of his passion and death, and in the fourth "week" he or she desires to share Jesus' joy in his resurrection. Each "week" lasts as long as it takes for the retreatant to attain from God the grace desired.

Because his lack of theological training got him into trouble with the Inquisition of the time, Ignatius, as he later preferred to call himself, decided to get a formal education in philosophy and theology and eventually went to the University of Paris. Here he met and became friends with other students, men like Francis Xavier, Pierre Favre, Nicholas Bobadilla, Alfonso Salmeron, and Diego Laynez. He directed each of them individually through the Exercises, and each of them decided to follow Christ unreservedly as did Ignatius. When these students made the Exercises they ranged in age from about eighteen to twenty-five. These young men were the founders of the Society of Jesus. I hope that it helps to dispel the mystique of the Spiritual Exercises to realize both how young these men were and that all but one were laymen at the time of making the Exercises.

What are the Spiritual Exercises? Here's what Ignatius himself says:

> By the term "Spiritual Exercises" is meant every
> method of examination of conscience, of meditation,

13

of contemplation, of vocal and mental prayer, and of other spiritual activities that will be mentioned later. For just as taking a walk, journeying on foot, and running are bodily exercises, so we call Spiritual Exercises every way of preparing and disposing the soul to rid itself of all inordinate attachments, and, after their removal, of seeking and finding the will of God in the disposition of our life for the salvation of our soul (*Spiritual Exercises* n. 1).

What Ignatius seems to mean, then, by spiritual exercises are any means by which we come into contact with God: means to overcome our resistances and to relate to God and, in the relating, to discover and to try to live out God's hopes for us. These Exercises are ways of meeting God and of discerning in our experience what is of God and what is not of God. Let's try to spell out some of Ignatius' presuppositions.

First, Ignatius learned from his own experience that God, the holy Mystery who is three in one, not only wants a personal relationship with each person both as an individual and as a community, but also acts in this world to bring about such a personal relationship. Indeed, one can argue that the Ignatian Exercises rest on the theological assumption that God creates this universe precisely in order to invite other persons into the relational life of the Trinity. God's purpose or intention of inviting each person into the relational life of the Trinity is not episodic, occurring periodically in each person's life. God is always acting to bring about this intention.

Another way of making the same point is to say that God is always in conscious relationship with each one of us as our creator, our sustainer, dear father or dear mother, our brother, our savior, the Spirit who dwells in our hearts. Ignatius presupposes that at every moment of our existence God is communicating to us who God is, is trying to draw us into an awareness, a consciousness of the reality of who we are in God's sight. Whether we are aware of it or not, at every moment of our existence we are encountering God,

Father, Son, and Holy Spirit, who is trying to catch our attention, trying to draw us into a reciprocal conscious relationship.

Second, the Spiritual Exercises are ways of helping us to become more aware of the reality of our existence as the objects of God's communication. Experience is an encounter between a being that exists and a person capable of being conscious of the encounter.[2] Faith tells us that God exists both as transcendent to and immanent in this world. So God is encountered. But we are not always conscious of, or alert to, the presence of God. The religious dimension of experience is supplied not only by the God who exists and is encountered, but also by a person of faith on the alert for God. The various exercises contained in the book of *The Spiritual Exercises* have as their purpose to heighten our awareness, to sharpen our ability to feel the "finger of God." These Exercises, then, are for anyone who wants to sharpen that awareness.

Perhaps some examples will make this more concrete. For the past several years, James Skehan, S.J., professor of geology and geophysics at Boston College, has been directing groups of people through the full Spiritual Exercises while they continue their ordinary lives. The retreat lasts about twenty-four weeks. Each retreatant takes time for prayer and reflection each day. In addition, they meet as a group for liturgy, dinner, and sharing of experience once a week. At the end of the latest retreat, I asked past and present participants to give me some reflections about what had happened. The retreatants have been faculty members, staff, graduate and undergraduate students, former students, and other people from the area, a cross section of the church, you might say.

One person wrote:

> The most powerful concept that occurred to me was that
> I am an actual member of the body of Christ and

can participate with him in the transformation of the world. . . . Because I am a member of the body of Christ I am more aware of my own dignity and also of the presence of God in all people and all things.

Another said: "Perhaps the single greatest fruit of this retreat has been to discover what the Spirit wants me to do in following Jesus." A third wrote:

Somehow, I cannot imagine that I will ever be the same person who started this retreat. My spiritual life up to then consisted of traditional prayer, often said without much thought. . . . These past several months of reflection and prayer I feel have become a very special part of me. The first reaction at this moment is to say that I am not afraid to die. Mind you now, I don't wish to die one second before my time. What I mean is that I never before was able to reflect on death and see what might be the beginning of a better life and not just the end of a good one.

A fourth wrote:

Silence and solitude now have meaning; they are no longer a space to be filled with activity or words but a time to listen and rest in peace and an ever-increasing sense of being loved. I now listen with a new awareness of every individual, and each interaction is not an isolated occurrence but a part of an ongoing conversation intending nothing less than that lovely Ignatian notion of seeing God in all things. Concretely I find myself smiling and laughing more often in the presence of others. . . . I feel my life is no longer an independent pursuit, for I must continually reach out in recognition of this human community.

These are wonderful testimonies to the power of the Spiritual Exercises in our own day.

Third among the presuppositions Ignatius makes is that the most important prerequisite for using at least some of these exercises is the desire to become more aware of the presence of God in one's life and to develop one's conscious relationship with this self-communicating God. One does not need any theological sophistication. Ignatius, as mentioned, was theologically illiterate when he first began the conscious development of his relationship with God. Nor does one need to be holy or even relatively far advanced in the spiritual life to make use of these exercises. Ignatius was, by his own admission, a spiritual child when he began the exercises at Manresa. In spite of these lacks, however, Ignatius had the one thing necessary to undertake the journey, namely great desires. He distilled this concept in the fifth annotation at the beginning of *The Spiritual Exercises*:

> It will be very profitable for the one who is to go through the Exercises to enter upon them with magnanimity and generosity toward his Creator and Lord, and to offer him his entire will and liberty, that his Divine Majesty may dispose of him and all he possesses according to his most holy will (*Spiritual Exercises* n. 5).

I take magnanimity and generosity to mean great desires and also great expectations of what God wants to give me during this period.

Fourth, Ignatius presupposes that the path through the Exercises will not be smooth. In fact, in the sixth annotation Ignatius tells the director to question carefully any retreatant who "is not affected by any spiritual experiences, such as consolations or desolations, and . . . is not troubled by different spirits" (*Spiritual Exercises* n. 6). Ignatius began his own conversion when he noted the different emotional reactions caused by the two sets of daydreams, and he came to the conclusion that our hearts are something like a battleground. Not only is God trying to engage us in a dialogical relationship, but the evil one is also trying to draw us away from that relationship. If we give ourselves a chance to become aware of God's communications through making the Spiritual Exercises, we also open ourselves to the counterattractions of the evil one. We will, therefore, experience

17

internal ups and downs. So another prerequisite for making the Exercises is the ability to notice and talk about what
happens interiorly while one is doing them. In the process of
noticing and talking about these various movements of our
hearts we will have to learn to discern in our experiences
what is of God from what is not of God.

One retreatant described the process of discernment in
this way:

> I am extremely grateful that this retreat has brought
> an increase in my awareness of the abiding presence of
> God, and has done so by directing my attention to the
> only moment I have at any time, the present one. This
> has been reinforced by St. Ignatius' wise words to exam-
> ine the day and what is moving through it in terms of
> spiritual light or spiritual darkness. All this is extremely
> important for me to practice because I would rather
> hope to find God in big and exciting events — yet
> then I would miss him in the simple and little events of
> each day.

The fact that the one who makes the full Spiritual Exercises has to be able to notice and talk about his or her inner
life implies something about the relationship between the
individual and the director of the Exercises. Sensible people
will reveal their inner lives only to people they trust. Hence,
the director of the Spiritual Exercises has to be a person who
can be trusted. The trust obviously includes confidentiality
and an ability to help with the relationship with God. But
the director also has to be a "skilled helper," a person who
knows how to help another to explore inner experience and
to recognize emerging desires.[3] Moreover, the director needs
to be someone who can adapt the Exercises to the needs and
talents of the individual.

Many people think of the Spiritual Exercises as a planned
and relatively fixed program of exercises to which a person
submits. Indeed, many of us older people experienced the
Ignatian Exercises in precisely this way. Those of us who

18

made the full Exercises of thirty days prior to 1965 or so made them in groups. The director gave four or five talks each day in which he set out the matter for prayer for the four or five hours of prayer. There was little chance for individual direction because of the size of the groups. As a result there was a sort of lock-step movement through the thirty days. Until it was shown that originally the Spiritual Exercises were individually directed and only later adapted for groups, there were many who felt that the individually directed Exercises were a modern aberration.

Yet it was the genius of Ignatius to write a book that could be adapted to all sorts of people according to both their desires and capabilities and their availability. Ignatius put it this way:

> The Spiritual Exercises must be adapted to the condition of the one who is to engage in them, that is, to his age, education, and talent. Thus exercises that he could not easily bear, or from which he would derive no profit, should not be given to one with little natural ability or of little physical strength. Similarly, each one should be given those exercises that would be more helpful and profitable according to his willingness to dispose himself for them.
>
> Hence, one who wishes no further help than some instruction and the attainment of a certain degree of peace of soul may be given the Particular Examination of Conscience. . . .
>
> Similarly, if the one giving the Exercises sees that the exercitant has little aptitude or little physical strength, that he is one from whom little fruit is to be expected, it is more suitable to give him some of the easier exercises as a preparation for confession (*Spiritual Exercises* n. 18).

Adaptation is the name of the game, and the director of the Exercises has to be someone who has the art to make the appropriate adaptations to the persons involved.

Another misconception is that you have to go away to

a retreat house in the country to make the Spiritual Exercises. Yet Ignatius gave the Spiritual Exercises to his first companions in the middle of the turbulent "Left Bank" of Paris. I have directed people in the full Exercises who lived in Boston and took the subway to see me each day. An acre of woods or seashore is not necessary to meet God.

Moreover, Ignatius conceived of a way for a person who could not take thirty days off from work to make the full Spiritual Exercises. In the 19th Annotation he writes: "One who is educated or talented, but engaged in public affairs or necessary business, should take an hour and a half daily for the Spiritual Exercises" (*Spiritual Exercises* n. 19). Many people have made the full Exercises in this manner. They meet their director every week or every two weeks over a period of about thirty weeks. Thousands of people in Canada and the United States have made the full Exercises in this way in the past twenty years. A person can also make part of the full Exercises in this manner.

One of the hallmarks of Ignatian spirituality is the belief that God can be found in all things. Ignatius believed that we encounter God at every moment of our existence. The Spiritual Exercises are various methods to help us to become more and more aware of this ever-present God. If we want to, we can become contemplatives in action, people who are alert to God's presence in all our daily activities.

FOOTNOTES

1. See *The Autobiography of St. Ignatius Loyola.* Ed. John C. Olin, Tr. Joseph F. O'Callaghan (New York: Harper & Row, 1974), pp. 22–24.

2. Here I rely on John E. Smith, *Experience and God* (New York: Oxford, 1968).

3. See Gerard Egan, *The Skilled Helper: A Systematic Approach to Effective Helping*, 3rd ed. (Monterey, CA: Brooks/Cole, 1986).

CHAPTER 1

"Can I Trust God?":
Healing Life's Hurts

A few years ago I heard a rather sick joke. A father puts his five-year-old son Sammy on a ten-foot-high wall. "Jump, Sammy, I'll catch you." "I'm scared." "Trust your father, Sammy, jump. I'll catch you." Finally after much cajoling, Sammy jumps and his father steps aside. "That's a lesson for you, Sammy. Never trust anyone." Sammy won't forget that lesson in a hurry, will he? Many people go through life with hurts and resentments that make it very difficult to trust life and the future and the author of life.

The Spiritual Exercises presume a desire on the part of a person to relate to God more intimately. They are various ways to uncover our resistances and disorders in order to relate more openly to God and, in the relating, to discover and to try to live out God's hopes for us.

Many people with an interest in religion have been traumatized by life and perhaps by false or inaccurate teachings about God. Their image of God is such that all they want is to keep on his right side or to keep as far away from God as possible. At most such people might have the desire to want to get to know God more intimately. Something has to happen to them before they can enter the full process of the Spiritual Exercises. Since the Spiritual Exercises include many ways of relating to God, however, even such preliminary attempts to get over the effect of traumatic events on one's image of God are spiritual exercises.

When Ignatius went to Paris to study, he roomed with Pierre Favre and Francis Xavier, both young students in their early twenties. Pierre Favre quickly came under the influence of Ignatius. But Ignatius did not direct him through the full Spiritual Exercises until four years had passed. Pierre was full of scruples, terrified of God's wrath. He seems to have had an image of God as a terrifying snoop seeking to catch him out. With such an image of God he could not enter the Spiritual Exercises with trust and hope and great desires for closeness to God. Who would want to get close to an all-powerful snoop or policeman? But Ignatius worked patiently and kindly with him during the four years and gradually Pierre's image of God changed and his scruples disappeared. He now desired closeness to God and wanted to know what God's hopes and plans for him were. Ignatius led him through the Spiritual Exercises, and Pierre decided to join Ignatius as a companion. He was one of the ten founders of the Society of Jesus and was considered by Ignatius to be the best director of the Spiritual Exercises among all of the first Jesuits.

Many people have an image of God that keeps them in continual anxiety. The British psychoanalyst Henry Guntrip notes:

> It is a common experience in psychotherapy to find patients who fear and hate God, a God who, in the words of J. S. Mackenzie, "is always snooping around after sinners," and who "becomes an outsize of the threatening parent. . . . The child grows up fearing evil rather than loving good; afraid of vice rather than in love with virtue."[1]

Our image of God takes its root in our childhood experiences and in the teaching about God which as children

22

we can easily garble in our psyches. People who have been abused physically, psychically, or sexually may carry around gravely distorted images of themselves in relation to author-ity figures and especially to God. I recall one woman who could not open the Bible without finding condemnations of herself. Scrupulous people live in continual anxiety of com-mitting serious sin for the most trivial of faults. God really is a snoop and a tyrant for them. Such people need much pa-tient help to let God change the image they have of him. Often enough the image begins to change when they can ad-mit that they do "hate" this God. Once I asked a man who lived in such fear of a tyrant God, "Do you like this God?" He blurted out, "No, I hate him." I replied: "I don't blame you; who wouldn't hate such a tyrant?" This outburst was the beginning of a change in his image of God and of him-self in relation to God, but even then it took a long time for the change of image to take strong enough root so that he could banish the scrupulous, obsessive ruminations. I came to believe that the anger and rage against the tyrant God emanated from the Spirit of God railing against such a per-verted image.

Many people have also been hurt badly by tragedies that life often brings in its train. A dearly loved mother dies young of cancer. A brother is killed by a drunken driver. A teenager is paralyzed from the waist down in a football game. If God is so good, how can God let such things happen? Peo-ple who have suffered such tragedies can easily empathize with Job who is, seemingly, tossed on a dare to the whims of Satan by God.

> Then the Lord said to Satan, "Have you considered my servant Job? There is no one on earth like him; he is blameless and upright, a man who fears God and shuns evil."
> "Does Job fear God for nothing?" Satan replied. "Have you not put a hedge around him and his house-hold and everything he has?. . . But stretch out your

23

hand and strike everything he has, and he will surely
curse you to your face."
    The Lord said to Satan, "Very well, then, everything
he has is in your hands, but on the man himself do not
lay a finger" (Job 1:8–12).

Job lost everything including all his children, and then on
another dare from Satan, God allowed Satan to cover him
with scabs and boils. "After this, Job opened his mouth and
cursed the day of his birth" (Job 3:1). In the book Job moves
back and forth from angry complaints about God to expres-
sions of great hope and trust in God. "The arrows of the
Almighty are in me, my spirit drinks in their poison; God's
terrors are marshaled against me" (6:4). "Though I cry, 'I've
been wronged!' I get no response; though I call for help,
there is no justice" (19:7). "I know that my Redeemer lives,
and that in the end he will stand upon the earth. And after
my skin has been destroyed, yet in my flesh I will see God. I
myself will see him with my own eyes — I, and not another.
How my heart yearns within me" (19:25–27).
    So too those who have suffered tragedies may have
to vent their rage and anger at their losses and even
confront the One whom they believe ultimately responsible.
They may find courage to speak their hearts out to God by
reading the Book of Job, especially chapters 23 and 24 which
begin:

> Even today my complaint is bitter;
> his hand is heavy in spite of my groaning.
> If only I knew where to find him;
>   if only I could go to his dwelling!
> I would state my case before him
>   and fill my mouth with arguments.
> I would find out what he would answer me,
>   and consider what he would say.
> Would he oppose me with great power?
> No, he would not press charges against me.
> There an upright man could present his case
>   before him,

and I would be delivered forever from my judge
(23:2–7).

Job held nothing back.

I recall a young woman who was preparing for her marriage. Her father had been killed in an accident when she
was ten. At the time she had grieved bitterly and for a whole
year had gone through the motions of living. But then she
seemed to get over the grief and her life progressed rather
happily. She prayed regularly, but God was a somewhat shad-
owy and distant figure. One day she stopped by the church
where her marriage would take place and sat down to reflect.
She began to fantasize about her wedding. She thought of
walking down the aisle with her uncle, her father's brother.
Suddenly she felt an anger billow up in her and she almost
yelled aloud, "No, I'll walk down that aisle by myself. I'll
show the world and you what you did to me when you took
my father!" Words came tumbling out as she told God in no
uncertain terms how angry, even enraged, she was against
him. She didn't want anything to do with him. When she
told me the story, I asked how she felt afterwards. She said
that she felt better, relieved. I asked whether she had a sense
of God's presence and how God seemed. She said that he
seemed to listen and to sympathize with her. In fact, since
that day she felt that God was much closer to her.

Sometimes people need to speak out their anger at life's
hurts and tragedies before they can come to a trusting and
warm relationship with God. Job provides a good example
of this kind of angry demand on God. Over and over he
protested that he had been unjustly treated. Over and over
he asked God to speak to him and to explain to him how
these tragedies could have happened to him. Finally in chapters 38 through 41 God does speak out of the whirlwind.
God did not offer cheap comfort nor did God justify what
had happened to Job. God just told Job who God is. However we may read these words of God, Job was comforted

by them. God had spoken directly to him. "My ears had heard of you but now my eyes have seen you. Therefore I despise myself and repent in dust and ashes" (42:5–6). Moreover, God expressed his anger at Job's friend and his approbation of Job's conduct toward God. God said to Eliphaz, "I am angry with you and your two friends, because you have not spoken of me what is right, as my servant Job has" (42:7). When people do speak their honest feelings of rage and anger to God, they often find God listening sympathetically, desirous to hear them out.

Here's another example from scripture. In the tenth chapter of Mark's gospel we read about the blind beggar Bartimaeus. Try to imagine what it might be like for Bartimaeus. Let's use our imaginations to flesh out this story, in the way Ignatius, in the Spiritual Exercises, encourages people to use their imaginations with scripture in order to let God communicate with them.

Suppose that Bartimaeus was born with sight and then lost it through a freak accident at the age of ten. His parents were poor, and so he had to leave whatever schooling he had and was forced to beg for a living. How would Bartimaeus feel about life and, perhaps, about the author of life? When he heard that Jesus, the healer, was near, he could have reacted with cynicism. Perhaps, in fact, his first cries, "Jesus, Son of David, have mercy on me!" were more in hope of a handout than a cure. Then Jesus calls him over and says to him: "What do you want me to do for you?" In the gospel story Bartimaeus responds immediately: "Rabbi, I want to see."

In the same circumstances how many of us would have had such trust? I wonder about myself at least. "What if I let my hopes get raised and nothing happens?" "I never have gotten what I wanted just by asking. I've had to beg and cajole, and even then most people don't give me what I want. What if he can't or won't give me what I want?" "If

I do receive my sight, what will I do with myself? I know how to eke out a living as a blind beggar. How will I make a living as a sighted person?" "I didn't ask to go blind. It wasn't my fault. I want some kind of apology from God for what happened to me before I'll beg for a cure."

People who have been hurt by life may have any or all of these reactions when faced with the possibility of turning to God with faith and hope and trust. They need help to voice their reactions to God and to see such speaking as valid prayer. Only after voicing their complaints and finding God still sympathetic will they be able to ask for healing from the hurts of life. "Rabbi, I want to see."

The healing of life's hurts can take a long time, especially if these hurts occurred in childhood. It took four years of patient pastoral care by Ignatius before Pierre Favre was sufficiently grounded in the experience of a loving creator to be able to enter more deeply into the dynamic of the Spiritual Exercises. People can be perplexed and even disconcerted that one clean breast of their feelings of anger about what happened to them does not seem to end the matter. A young woman who has poured out her feelings about being sexually and physically abused by her father and has felt the healing comfort of a God who sympathizes may be amazed and depressed that a year later the feelings return and seem unabated. Experiences such as this happen often. The person comes to feel that things will never really change, that she is doomed to an endless cycle, like a hamster in a cage. It can be quite disheartening. Perhaps a few words about the process psychoanalysts call "working through" may help us to understand this phenomenon.

Repeatedly in psychoanalytic treatment clients have an "aha" experience, a deeply felt emotional insight into the process by which they defeat themselves. For example, John may realize that he has begun to denigrate the analyst just as he has denigrated most of his superiors at work because he has become afraid that the analyst will reject him. At work his attitude leads to subtle and pernicious office gossip between himself and others that finally makes the place intolerable, and he is either fired or passed over for promotion. In the analysis he recognizes with great relief that he does not have to be afraid of the analyst or of his bosses, i.e., that they are not his father or mother.

It looks like smooth sailing from here on. But it is not so. Within the week he again begins to feel the same way toward the analyst, and the whole process has to be repeated. But usually with a difference. The second time he sees more of the motivation for his behavior, more of the complex, multivalent desires, fears, and impulses that determine his self-defeating reactions to his superiors. Psychoanalysts note that the resistance to insights such as these dies hard. It takes a lot of patient work by both analyst and client to bury resistance and have it stay (relatively) buried.

Our personalities are complex psychic structures which have evolved over all the years of our lives. Nothing significant in our life is totally lost; it has left its residue in our psyche. Thus, every new interaction with someone significant is colored by our past interactions. If I fall in love with someone, for example, at least some of my reactions to this person will be triggered by the psychic structures developed through loving interactions with other persons. When I am hurt by something this person does, as another example, at least some of my reactions stem from my past experiences of being hurt by loved ones.

The strength of our emotional responses in the present are often only explainable by the theory that our psyches are amalgams of all our past significant encounters. Moreover, we are often unaware that old wounds have been opened by a new relationship. In fact, we often strongly resist becoming aware because of the anxiety and pain such awareness would bring. If we do become aware, we have a habit of quickly blocking out its memory. Hence, the need to return again and again to the same issue in psychotherapy. The return is also to deeper and deeper levels of the psychic structure because most of the traumatic events that cause us trouble in present relationships occurred when we were children.

John, the psychoanalytic client mentioned above, has built up over years habitual ways of dealing with superiors, ways that have been reinforced by his repeated failures. That is, each time he was fired or missed a promotion reinforced the feelings of inadequacy that stemmed from childhood experiences of dealing with his parents. Again and again, at ever deeper levels, he must unlearn these reaction patterns, or, rather, he must learn new ways of reacting, ways that are more compatible with his present adult reality. But the old patterns die hard because they were developed to cope with overwhelming anxiety in childhood and were reinforced so often in adult life.

It is with such complex personality structures that we "ordinary" neurotics engage in life and also in our prayer life. Mike's relationship with Joe, for example, is colored by all his past close relationships. So when he is hurt by Joe, some of his emotional reaction derives from that past. Old wounds are opened. So too, for another example, Joan's reaction to Jesus is colored at least in part by her past experiences with those whom she loved and before whom she felt inadequate. We never have an experience, even an experience of God, that is not somehow tinged with the residues of our past experiences. Hence, the strength of our emotional reactions may often be more attributable to our past experiences than to the present triggering experience. But we are usually unaware of the influence of the past on our reactions.

Just as the analytic patient needs time to "work through" resistances to insight, so too we need time to "work through" our resistances to more adult, Christian behavior. Just as the analytic patient gradually comes to appropriate the insight and to react in new ways in spite of discouraging regressions, so too, if a person who has been hurt by life continues to ask the Lord for his healing, that healing will come. I do not believe that we have to unearth all of the psychic structures that condition present reactions and behavior. For one thing such archeology of the psyche would take a lifetime of digging. For another, the Lord heals us in hidden ways, and we do not need to know everything. What we need to do is to continue to put ourselves into his loving care to heal our wounds and bring us to a deep experience that we really are held in the arms of a loving creator.

One final example. Joan, a forty-year-old wife and mother, has had a very hard time believing that God or Jesus could love her as she is. On a retreat she had a profound experience of God's love which dispelled all her doubts that God could ever love and forgive her. She felt free and euphoric, a changed person who no longer, it seemed to her, would be prey to the self-doubts and fears that had periodically plagued her.

Three days after the retreat she began to pray and read the words of Jesus to the woman with the flow of blood, "Daughter, your faith has healed you" (Mk 5:34). She sensed Jesus' eyes on her and felt afraid, afraid that he saw too little faith. All her self-doubts returned, and she became very discouraged. What could she do?

I believe that Joan needs only to tell Jesus that his eyes seem angry and disappointed once again and ask him to help her to relive the experience of the retreat. Each time she feels lost and discouraged she repeats the request, and gradually she will discover that the periods of trust and confidence grow longer, the periods of doubt and confusion shorter. (It may, of course, be helpful to her also to seek counseling if there is a long history of depression. I am thinking of the ordinary lack of self-confidence most of us have when we face God.) If she does this, gradually Joan will allow the Spirit of the Lord to transform her psyche, to permeate more and more of its layers, and thus heal some of life's hurts. But the transformation can only happen if she does not deny the recurring feelings; that is, if she has a patient willingness to present herself to the Lord in all her brokenness.

Joan and the rest of us need to be willing to admit our reality into consciousness and to admit it to the Lord and to let the Lord's Spirit work through the hurts much as a baker kneads yeast into flour.

Ultimately, in order to desire with real passion more intimacy with God we need to love God, to be attracted to God. No one is attracted to a snoop or a tyrant. We need a deep experience of a God who really is attractive. Ignatius, it seems, bent all his efforts over a four-year period to help Pierre Favre come to the "enjoyment of God" described by the British psychiatrist J. S. Mackenzie cited earlier.

> The *enjoyment of God* should be the supreme end of spiritual technique; and it is in that enjoyment of God that we feel not only saved in the Evangelical sense, but safe: we are conscious of belonging to God, and hence are never alone; and, to the degree we have these two, hostile feelings disappear.... In that relationship Nature seems friendly and homely; even its vast spaces instead of eliciting a sense of terror speak of the infinite love; and the nearer beauty becomes the garment with which the Almighty clothes Himself.[2]

The next chapter will take up this foundational experience.

Questions for prayer and/or discussion:

1. Is there some area of my past life that needs healing? Can I tell God about it?
2. Have I ever felt angry at God? Can I tell God that? If I have told God about my anger, how did God seem to react?

FOOTNOTES

1. Henry Guntrip, *Psychotherapy and Religion* (New York: Harper, 1957), pp. 194–195. The citation of Mackenzie is from *Nervous Disorders and Character.*

2. *Ibid.*

CHAPTER 2

Grounded in God: The Principle and Foundation

How do we come to be attracted to God, to the enjoyment of God described by British psychiatrist J. S. Mackenzie quoted at the end of the last chapter? In this chapter I want to point out a possible direction for our reflections and prayer so that we might answer this question for ourselves.

The Baltimore Catechism asked the question: "Why did God make me?" and we memorized the answer: "God made me to know him, to love him, and to serve him and to be happy with him forever in heaven." At the beginning of *The Spiritual Exercises* Ignatius makes a similar statement in what he calls "The Principle and Foundation." "A human being is created to praise, reverence, and serve God our Lord, and by this means to save his or her soul" (*Spiritual Exercises* n. 23). A more modern translation runs: "Every person in the world is so put together that by praising, revering, and living according to the will of God our Lord he or she will safely reach the Reign of God. This is the original purpose of each human life."[1] These are, however, rather dry, even if theologically impeccable, statements. As such they cannot ground a life and a developing relationship with God.

We do not know and love and serve an abstraction. To ground a life and a relationship, these statements must be the distillation of experience. Moreover, it has to be an experience that is universal, that is had in some fashion or other by every person who lives. In other words, if these statements are true, then every person must be able to have an experience that draws him or her to the knowledge, love, and service of God. What is that experience?

Let me give you some examples. In *Let This Mind Be in You*, Sebastian Moore suggests that we all have experiences of desiring "I know not what," experiences which are also accompanied by a feeling of great well-being. He believes that these experiences are experiences of being touched by the creative desire of God who desires us into being and continues us in being. "God could be defined — or rather pointed to — by this experience, as that which . . . causes in us that desire for we know not what, which is the foundational religious experience."[2] He refers to C. S. Lewis' autobiography *Surprised by Joy*, where Lewis describes such an experience:

> As I stood before a flowering currant bush on a summer day there suddenly arose in me without warning, and as if from a depth not of years but of centuries, the memory of that earlier morning at the Old House when my brother had brought his toy garden into the nursery. It is difficult to find words strong enough for the sensation which came over me; Milton's "enormous bliss" of Eden . . . comes somewhere near it. It was a sensation, of course, of desire; but desire for what? not, certainly, for a biscuit tin filled with moss, nor even (though that came into it) for my own past . . . and before I knew what I desired, the desire itself was gone, the whole glimpse withdrawn, the world turned commonplace again, or only stirred by a longing for the longing that had just ceased. It had taken only a moment of time; and in a certain sense everything else that had ever happened to me was insignificant in comparison.[3]

34

Bernard Berenson mentions times when he lost himself in "some instant of perfect harmony."

> In childhood and boyhood this ecstasy overtook me when I was happy out of doors. Was I five or six? Certainly not seven. It was a morning in early summer. A silver haze shimmered and trembled over the lime trees. The air was laden with their fragrance. The temperature was like a caress. I remember — I need not recall — that I climbed up a tree stump and felt suddenly immersed in Itness. I did not call it by that name. I had no need for words. It and I were one.[4]

Admiral Byrd describes the following experience in the Antarctic in 1934:

> Took my daily walk at 4 p.m. today in eighty-nine degrees of frost. . . . I paused to listen to the silence. . . . The day was dying, the night being born — but with great peace. Here were imponderable processes and forces of the cosmos, harmonious and soundless. Harmony, that was it! . . .
> It was enough to catch that rhythm, momentarily to be myself a part of it. In that instant I could feel no doubt of man's oneness with the universe. The conviction came that that rhythm was too orderly, too harmonious, too perfect to be a product of blind chance — that, therefore, there must be purpose in the whole and that man was part of that whole and not an accidental off-shoot. It was a feeling that transcended reason; that went to the heart of man's despair and found it groundless.[5]

Lest we think that such experiences are reserved only for brilliant and important people, let me refer to a scene in Anne Tyler's novel *Dinner at the Homesick Restaurant*. Pearl Tull is an old, blind, dying woman who was abandoned by her husband and who brought up three children alone. She lives with one of her sons, Ezra, and his task each day is to read to her some of her diary from her childhood. Most of the entries are pretty banal, and Pearl quickly has him move

on. Then comes the final scene before her death. Ezra riffles
through some entries and begins to read:

> "Early this morning," he read to his mother, "I went
> out behind the house to weed. Was kneeling in the
> dirt by the stable with my pinafore a mess and perspira-
> tion rolling down my back, wiped my face on my sleeve,
> reached for the trowel, and all at once thought, Why I
> believe that at just this moment I am absolutely happy."
>   His mother stopped rocking and grew still.
>   "The Bedloe girl's piano scales were floating out her
> window," he read, "and a bottle fly was buzzing in the
> grass, and I saw that I was kneeling on such a beautiful
> green little planet. I don't care what else might come
> about, I have had this moment. It belongs to me."
>   That was the end of the entry. He fell silent.
>   "Thank you, Ezra," his mother said. "There's no
> need to read any more."[6]

Obviously Pearl wanted to remember that foundational experience once more before she died.

Perhaps too Wordsworth was referring to such an experience of desire for "I know not what" in this poem:

> My heart leaps up when I behold
>   A rainbow in the sky:
> So was it when my life began;
> So is it now I am a man;
> So be it when I shall grow old,
>   Or let me die!
> The Child is father of the Man;
> And I could wish my days to be
> Bound each to each by natural piety.

Notice that these experiences do not have to be interpreted theologically, as experiences of God. Berenson, for
example, speaks of Itness. Pearl Tull does not speak of God.
But a believer can interpret such experiences as these as experiences of the creative touch of God. In order to draw out
the implications of such experiences we need to reflect on
them.

First we need to notice that the experiences speak of desire. The experience seems to be for union with "I know not what," with mystery, with the all. C. S. Lewis makes the point most clearly, but one can sense the strength of desire in each of the experiences cited — and in our own experiences. We want something very much, and the desire is not for this or that thing or even for health or happiness, but for relationship, for union.

Next we notice that the experience includes a sense of great well-being. While in the experience we do not worry about ourselves, our worth, our goodness. We seem to take for granted that we are okay in so far as we think of ourselves at all. We feel right with the world, as it were. Moore interprets the experience, quite rightly, as an experience of being desired into existence by God. Hence we are desirable.[7]

We might, however, miss the most significant aspect of the experience if we do not reflect further. The experiences speak of something happening now, not of something that happened in the past. Often enough when we think of our creation or of the creation of the universe, we think of something that happened long ago. We imagine that God started the universe eons ago. Even if we imagine God creating us, we tend to think of our creation as happening when we were conceived or born. But the experiences we have been discussing are described as having happened in the present. Even when they are remembered, the memory is of an experience. Lewis, Berenson, Byrd, and Pearl Tull describe experiences they had during their lives. If these are experiences of the creative touch of God, then we are talking of an action of God that is going on continually, not of an action that happened in some distant point in time. When we have such experiences, we are experiencing the present action of God.

What can this mean? With the philosopher John Macmurray we can consider the universe as one action of God. Let me illustrate what he means by an action. This book on Ignatian prayer is one action of mine because it is governed by one intention. I want to present Ignatius' spirituality over the course of this book in such a way that it will have an influence on my readers. This one action includes many other actions and many events not under my control, including your interest in the book and its subject. Thus this book is one action.

In an analogous way we can understand the universe as one action of God. Given this understanding God is continually doing his one action which is the universe. Hence, God is always active, always doing his thing, as it were. Thus, at every moment of existence God is creating this world and everything in it.

Now we noted that an action is defined by its intention. What does God intend with this one action which is the universe? We only know the intentions of persons (and only persons can perform actions) if they reveal them to us. For example, in a court of law people are not required to testify against themselves by revealing their intentions. The judge and jury have to come to a judgment on the basis of circumstantial evidence. They infer intention when they conclude that the person is guilty. But they can be mistaken. Certainty about the intentions of persons can only come if the persons reveal their intentions truthfully.

If this is true of human beings, how much more true of God! We can only know God's intention for the one action that is the universe if God chooses to reveal it to us. Of course, Christians believe that God has revealed his intention. God, it seems, creates this universe to invite all persons to enter the community life of the Trinity, the perfect community of Father, Son, and Holy Spirit. Another way of putting the same revelation is to say that God's intention is the reign of God proclaimed by Jesus. God wants all persons to live as sisters and brothers of Jesus in harmony with the whole created universe. The Letter to the Ephesians puts it this way:

> Praise be to the God and Father of our Lord Jesus Christ, who has blessed us in the heavenly realms with every spiritual blessing in Christ. For he chose us in him before the creation of the world to be holy and blameless in his sight. In love he predestined us to be adopted as his sons and daughters through Jesus Christ, in accordance with his pleasure and will — to the praise of his glorious grace, which he has freely given us in the One he loves.... And he made known to us the mystery of his will according to his good pleasure, which he purposed in Christ, to be put into effect when the times will have reached their fulfillment — to bring all things in heaven and on earth together under one head, even Christ (Eph 1:3–6, 9–10).[8]

Thus, I would argue, when we have foundational experiences such as I described earlier, we are experiencing the creative action of God which is always at work to bring us and all persons into the reign of God, into the community of the Trinity. We may not draw out all the implications of such experiences, but nonetheless, I believe that we can do so. In fact, Ignatius has drawn out these implications from his own mystical experiences and distilled them in the Principle and Foundation.[9] When we experience the desire for "I know not what," we are experiencing God's one creative action which calls each one of us and the whole universe into being with the intention of drawing all persons into the one community which is the Trinity. No wonder C. S. Lewis could say that he was "surprised by joy," by a desire that "had taken only a moment of time" but which made "everything else that had ever happened to me . . . insignificant in comparison."

Let's take a further step in our reflections. When I have the experience of desiring I know not what, I am experiencing God creating me *now* in all the particulars of my present existence. While immersed in the experience I do not worry about my past failures and sins or about what the future will hold. I feel at one with the universe and as whole as I could possibly be. Moreover, the desire I experience is the deepest desire within me. That desire is in tune with God's one intention in creating the universe, and that desire can become the ruling passion of my life, if I let it. I believe that this desire comes from the Holy Spirit who dwells in our hearts. I am reminded of Paul's words in the Letter to the Romans:

> We know that the whole creation has been groaning as in the pains of childbirth right up to the present time. Not only so, but we ourselves, who have the firstfruits of the Spirit, groan inwardly as we wait eagerly for our adoption as sons, the redemption of our bodies. For in this hope we were saved. But hope that is seen is no hope at all. Who hopes for what he already has? But if we hope for what we do not yet have, we wait for it patiently.
>
> In the same way, the Spirit helps us in our weakness. We do not know what we ought to pray for, but the Spirit himself intercedes for us with groans that words cannot express. And he who searches our hearts knows the mind of the Spirit, because the Spirit intercedes for the saints in accordance with God's will (Rom 8:22–27).

When we experience the desire for "I know not what," it is God's Holy Spirit drawing us into the community which is the Trinity.

This deepest desire of our hearts is for God. While we are in the throes of this desire, everything else we might desire takes a back seat, as it were. Everything else becomes relative before the absolute Mystery we desire. Moreover, insofar as this desire reigns in our hearts, we also desire to live

out our lives in harmony with this desire. Hence we want
to live in harmony with God's creative purpose for us, to
choose what will be more in tune with our desire for union
with God. Ignatius spells out the implications of the foundational experience of God's creative touch in the Principle
and Foundation. Here is Tetlow's version:

> Every person in the world is so put together that by
> praising, revering, and living according to the will of
> God our Lord he or she will safely reach the Reign of
> God. This is the original purpose of each human life.
>
> Every other thing on the face of the earth is meant
> for humankind, to help each person come to the original
> purpose God has put in each of us.
>
> The only thing that makes sense in the use of all
> other things, then, is that a person use everything that
> helps realize that original purpose deep in the self, and
> turn away from everything that alienates us from the
> original purpose in ourself.
>
> We can push this a little further: When we are
> under no obligations in conscience, we ought to keep
> ourselves free of any fixed preference for one or other
> created thing. Instead, we ought to keep ourselves at
> balance before anything. What does this entail? It means
> that before we ever face any decision we do not deter-
> mine to do everything that will keep us healthy and
> nothing that might make us sick, to be rich rather than
> poor, to be considered somebody important rather than
> a nobody, to live to a very old age rather than to die
> younger. In that way, we would keep a balance before
> any created thing when the times come for decision.
>
> We set ourselves to live in careful balance, to want
> to choose solely on the grounds of what leads
> more directly and more certainly to our original
> purpose.[10]

Tetlow uses the phrase "at balance" as a translation of
what most other translations term "indifference." The term
"indifference" can give the impression that Ignatius wants
people who do not care for the things of this world. The

term "at balance" comes much closer to Ignatius' intent. In the throes of the desire for "I know not what" we do not want anything else to get in the way of the fulfillment of that deepest desire. Thus before every choice that we have in life we want to be at balance in order to discern or discover what will more surely bring us what we most deeply desire. Another typical Ignatian concept is the word "more" or *magis* in Latin. We desire what will *more* directly and *more* certainly lead to our original purpose.

I believe that the experience of this desire for "I know not what" is the universal experience we were seeking that would ground the catechism answer and the Principle and Foundation of Ignatius. Not everyone who has the experience will make it the touchstone of their lives. But to those who want to make it such Ignatius offers the Spiritual Exercises.

Questions for prayer and/or discussion:

1. Have I had any experiences like the ones described? Have these experiences supported me in my prayer life? If I haven't paid much attention to them, do I now want to let them ground a renewed relationship with God?
2. Would I like to live "at balance"? What would that mean for me?

FOOTNOTES

1. The translation is by Joseph A. Tetlow, S.J., *Choosing Christ in the World: Directing the Spiritual Exercises of St. Ignatius Loyola According to Annotations Eighteen and Nineteen: A Handbook* (St. Louis, MO: The Institute of Jesuit Sources, 1989), p. 128.

2. Sebastian Moore, *Let This Mind Be in You: The Quest for Identity Through Oedipus to Christ* (Minneapolis, Chicago, New York: Winston, 1985), p. 36.

3. C. S. Lewis, *Surprised by Joy: The Shape of My Early Life* (London: Geoffrey Bles, 1955), p. 22.

4. Bernard Berenson, *Sketch for a Self-Portrait* (Bloomington, IN: Indiana University Press, 1958), p. 18.

5. Richard E. Byrd, *Alone* (New York: G. P. Putnam's Sons, 1938), pp. 84–85. The citations from Berenson and Byrd were first brought to my attention by Anthony Storr in his book *Solitude: A Return to the Self* (New York: Ballantine, 1988).

6. Anne Tyler, *Dinner at the Homesick Restaurant* (New York: Berkley Books, 1983), p. 284.

7. Moore, *op. cit.*

8. I have developed some of these ideas in *Paying Attention to God: Discernment in Prayer* (Notre Dame, IN: Ave Maria Press, 1990), pp. 77–85.

9. In this section I draw on the recent monograph of Joseph Tetlow "The Fundamentum: Creation in the Principle and Foundation," *Studies in the Spirituality of Jesuits* 21, no. 4 (September 1989). "When I talk about creation here, I have in mind the *In principio* of John's prologue and the first chapter of Ephesians. Hence, I mean a different beginning, a beginning in no way limited by time or place but always ongoing in specific time and concrete place. When I talk about creation in these pages, I refer to God's constantly making each creature out of nothing at each moment of its existence, anteceding and causing all secondary causes" (4–5).

10. Tetlow, *Choosing Christ in the World*, *op. cit.*, p. 128.

CHAPTER 3

"Show Me Your Ways": How God Reveals Sin to Us

Psalm 139, the one which begins:

> O Lord, you have searched me and you know me.
> You know when I sit and when I rise;
> you perceive my thoughts from afar.

ends with these words:

> Search me, O God, and know my heart;
> test me and know my anxious thoughts.
> See if there is any offensive way in me,
> and lead me in the way everlasting.

Let's just think about these words for a moment. When we pray these words, we are asking God to reveal to us our sins and sinful tendencies. How many of us feel comfortable about doing that? "Have God tell me what's wrong with me? You have to be crazy. When a close friend tells me that he or she wants to tell me something about myself, my stomach does a sort of flip-flop and my mouth goes dry. I expect the worst. And you expect me to ask God to tell me the truth about myself!"

44

Because it is so difficult to ask anyone, even our best friend, to tell us the truth about ourselves, we need to know in our bones that we are loved by that person. We need to know that he or she will not willingly hurt us by the revelation of the truth, that, indeed, the truth will deepen our relationship. The same is true of our relationship with God. That is why it is important to spend so much time helping people to have a foundational experience of the God who creates us out of love, who desires us as the apple of his eye. People who have such an experience and savor it engage in something like a honeymoon period with God. Ignatius himself seems to have had such a period after his first conversion in the castle of Loyola.

> Without any cares he persevered in his reading and
> his good intentions, . . . taking great pleasure in those
> books (the life of Christ and the lives of the saints). . . .
> The greatest consolation he received was to look at the
> sky and the stars, which he often did and for a long
> time, because as a result he felt within himself a very
> great desire to serve Our Lord.[1]

Many people have such periods of real enjoyment of God. Prayer is relatively easy; God seems very close and tender. But then something happens to break up the honeymoon relationship.

In human relationships people sometimes begin to doubt their good fortune. "This can't be happening to me. I'm just kidding myself." For example, one begins to wonder whether a friend will still love me if he or she knows that I was once a heavy drinker and was arrested for drunken driving. Or, what if I were to tell her that I don't really like her mother? Honeymoons always end and then the two parties have to test out how much the friendship or marriage can take. Something similar can happen in the relationship with God. People begin to wonder whether it is all a psychological trick they have played on themselves. One woman described an experience of God's closeness after she had vented her anger at God. It seemed that God said to her: "I love who you are. You are part of my Godness as I am a part of you." She said that she spent the next few days in a sort of drunken grace and total peace. Then, however, she found herself trying to explain it all away as a psychological phenomenon. But she said, "I know it wasn't. That's one reason I'm writing to you. To solidify it somehow. I have told a few trusted others." She also gladly gave me permission to quote her.

Some become aware of how sinful they have been and then can no longer believe that God would want to be that close to them. Simon Peter provides one good example. After the great draft of fish he "fell at Jesus' knees and said, 'Go away from me, Lord; I am a sinful man'" (Lk 5:8). At the epiphany of God which began Isaiah's mission, Isaiah cried out: "Woe to me. . . . I am ruined. For I am a man of unclean lips, and I live among a people of unclean lips, and my eyes have seen the King, the Lord Almighty" (Is 6:5). In the presence of the Holy Mystery we become acutely conscious of how unholy we are and of how much we are in need of forgiveness. When we have such experiences, we can understand the saints who felt more and more sinful the closer they came to God.

The interesting thing about this latter phenomenon, however, is that the experience of getting that close to God and feeling that unholy does not seem to have depressed the saints. Ignatius provides an interesting example. Early on in his days at Manresa when he was beginning the process of conversion he notes that a fever brought him to death's door. He "fully believed that his soul was about to leave him. At this a thought came to him telling him that he was just, but this caused him so much trouble that he rejected it and recalled his sins to mind."[2] A few months later on board ship such a severe storm arose that all aboard believed they were doomed. Ignatius says: "At this time, examining himself carefully and preparing to die, he was unable to be afraid of his sins or of being condemned, but he was greatly confused and sorrowful, as he believed he had not well used the gifts and graces which God had given him."[3] Then he reports the final time he was certain that he was about to die, in 1550. "At this time thinking about death, he felt such happiness and such spiritual consolation at having to die that he dissolved entirely into tears."[4] When God reveals our sins and sinful tendencies to us, we may well feel deep sorrow and even tears for what we have done, but we do not feel that God is gloating over us and is making us feel unworthy of his love and friendship. God's revelation of sin and sinful tendencies is enabling; it gives us courage to pick ourselves up and reform our lives.

The very opposite of that occurs when we take it upon ourselves to reform our lives. Ignatius tried it. The same ambition that led him to daydream of doing great knightly deeds in imitation of the heroes of the trashy romances he loved to read now led him to want to imitate all the austerities that the saints had engaged in. He took up terrible fasts, scourged himself, let his fingernails and hair grow unkempt, and in the process did permanent damage to his health. The result: an awful case of scruples and temptations which led him at one point to contemplate suicide.[5] Obsessive thoughts about sin which lead nowhere but to despair do not come from God. Ignatius eventually recognized that his scruples were a temptation, were actually worship of a false god.

I very much like the description Thomas Merton gives of the voice that led him finally to go to Mass.

> I will not easily forget how I felt that day. First, there was this sweet, strong, gentle, clean urge in me which said, "Go to Mass! Go to Mass!" It was something quite new and strange, this voice that seemed to prompt me, this firm, growing interior conviction of what I needed

to do. It had a suavity, a simplicity about it that I could not easily account for. And when I gave in to it, it did not exult over me, and trample me down in its raging haste to land its prey, but it carried me forward serenely and with purposeful direction.

That does not mean that my emotions yielded to it altogether quietly. I was really still a little afraid to go to a Catholic church of set purpose, with all the other people, and dispose myself in a pew, and lay myself open to the mysterious perils of that strange and powerful thing they called their "Mass."[6]

Merton here describes the way God appears when he reveals sin to one who desires that revelation.

Of course, with a person who is living a lie, for example, a married man cheating on his wife or a vowed religious having an affair, the intervention of God may be more upsetting. In such cases, as Ignatius notes in his rules for the discernment of spirits, God causes remorse of conscience and feelings of guilt (*Spiritual Exercises* n. 314). But even here the purpose is a conversion of life, not a binge of useless guilt feelings.

The Spiritual Exercises actually ask the retreatant to look at sin from the point of view of its cosmic and historical consequences. The retreatant who has imbibed the experience of the Principle and Foundation realizes that the world is not functioning as God intended. People do not live as brothers and sisters. Hatred seems much more prevalent than love. Murder, war, child abuse, ethnic, gender, and racial prejudice, and cruelty abound. What happened? The retreatant desires a deep understanding of what caused the malfunctioning of God's intention for the world. Ignatius puts the desire this way: "Here it will be to ask for shame and confusion, because I see how many have been lost on account of one mortal sin, and how many times I have deserved eternal damnation because of the many grievous sins I have committed" (*Spiritual Exercises* n. 48).

Ignatius then asks the retreatant to look at the sin of the angels, the first "I will not serve" which brought so much evil into the universe. Then he suggests a look at the sin of the first human beings, Adam and Eve, as recorded in the Book of Genesis, again an unwillingness to trust that what God wants is their happiness. Instead they trust the voice of the Evil One who tells them that God wants to keep them in subservience. They eat of the fruit of the tree of knowledge of good and evil and in consequence find themselves fearful of their nakedness before one another and before God. Where before, it seems, they enjoyed the intimate walks with God in the garden in the cool of the day, now they hide their nakedness and then lie to God. One of their sons, Cain, in a fit of jealousy kills his brother Abel. Almost immediately we see how fear and hatred enter the world of God's good creation because people could not believe that God had their best interests at heart. Finally Ignatius suggests that we consider the case of one person who willfully refuses the love of God and ends up in hell. This first meditation ends up with a heartfelt talk with Jesus on the cross:

> Imagine Christ our Lord present before you on the cross, and begin to speak with him, asking how it is that though he is Creator, he has stooped to become human, and to pass from eternal life to death here in time, that thus he might die for our sins. I shall reflect on myself and ask: "What have I done for Christ? What am I doing for Christ? What ought I to do for Christ?" As I behold Christ in this plight, nailed to the cross, I shall ponder what presents itself to my mind (*Spiritual Exercises* n. 53).

Ignatius then adds this note:

> The colloquy is made by speaking exactly as one friend speaks to another, or as a servant speaks to a master, now asking him for a favor, now blaming himself for some misdeed, now making known his affairs to him,

and seeking advice in them. Close with an Our Father
(*Spiritual Exercises* n. 54).

The important point about this first meditation on sin
and the suggestions about prayer are not so much the particulars of the sin of the angels and Adam and Eve, but rather
that sin has a history. Its effects live on in this universe and
these effects mar the universe God intended. Ignatius hopes
that the retreatant will receive a deep appreciation of the effects of sin by the grace of God and that the retreatant will
feel deep shame and confusion knowing his or her own complicity in this history of sin as a refusal to trust in God's plan
for his universe. And the suggestions for prayer indicate that
Ignatius expects an intimate conversation to develop between
the retreatant and God and Jesus. When we look on Jesus on
the cross with the deep awareness that the sins of humanity
have put him there, what do we see in his eyes? We could be
afraid that we will read in those eyes our condemnation, but
instead we see love and forgiveness. What is our response to
such self-sacrificing love? Ignatius wants us to tell Jesus our
reactions.

When I have directed people in the full Spiritual Exercises, I have most often asked them early in the retreat
to spend a day reviewing their lives as salvation history. It
is one way to recall the affective Principle and Foundation
that grounds their positive relationship with God. I suggest
that they ask God to reveal how God has been in their lives
since the beginning. Then I suggest that they recall a place
or a person of their early life and let the memories flood in,
almost like free association. During the day they can take
various periods of their lives and repeat the process. Most
often the day is a very positive experience.

Now as they consider the history of sin, Ignatius suggests
in the second meditation that they do something similar
to review their own history of sin. Here the desire is "for a
growing and intense sorrow for my sins" (*Spiritual Exercises*

50

n. 55). Then the retreatant goes over his or her life asking God to reveal how he or she has missed the mark (the translation of the Greek word for sin), fallen short of the glory of God, not lived up to the great hopes God has in creating him or her. Ignatius' meditation culminates in this fifth point.

> This is a cry of wonder accompanied by surging emotion as I pass in review all creatures. How is it that they have permitted me to live, and have sustained me in life! Why have the angels, though they are the sword of God's justice, tolerated me, guarded me, and prayed for me! Why have the saints interceded for me and asked favors for me! And the heavens, sun, moon, stars, and the elements; the fruits, birds, fishes, and other animals — why have they all been at my service! How is it that the earth did not open to swallow me up, and create new hells in which I should be tormented forever!
>
> Colloquy. I will conclude with a colloquy, extolling the mercy of God our Lord, pouring out my thoughts to him, and giving thanks to him that up to this very moment he has granted me life. I will resolve with his grace to amend for the future. Close with an Our Father (*Spiritual Exercises* nn. 60–61).

Obviously Ignatius expects that God will reveal our sins and sinful tendencies to us in such a way that we will actually be consoled. We are to have an increase of faith, hope, and love, be moved to tears of sorrow for our sins, but also to tears of love for a God who has been so good to us even though he knows us through and through, knows that we have not lived up to his hopes and dreams for us.

When we direct people in the Spiritual Exercises these days, we often use scripture texts to help them to encounter the forgiving God. Isaiah 43 is a case in point. The Israelites are in exile in Babylon, exiled because of their sins of idolatry. Their temple has been destroyed; they feel estranged from God and do not expect to hear a forgiving word. In this dark moment the prophet known as Second Isaiah speaks the word of Yahweh.

> Fear not, for I have redeemed you;
> I have summoned you by name; you are mine.
> When you pass through the waters, I will be
>   with you;
> and when you pass through the rivers,
> they will not sweep over you.
> When you walk through the fire, you will not be
>   burned;
> the flames will not set you ablaze.
> For I am the Lord, your God, the Holy One,
>   your Savior;
> . . .
> Since you are precious and honored in my sight,
> and because I love you,
> I give men in exchange for you,
> and people in exchange for your life.
> Do not be afraid, for I am with you (Is 43:2–5).

Imagine hearing those words spoken to you when you know how much you have fallen short of the hopes of God for you. Imagine the freedom and joy and perhaps tears of happiness that God loves you so much warts and all.

Another text that has a profound effect is the story of the woman caught in adultery at the beginning of the eighth chapter of John's gospel. "Woman," Jesus says, "where are they? Has no one condemned you?" "No one, sir," she said. "Then neither do I condemn you," he declared. "Go now and leave your life of sin" (Jn 8:9–11). The love of Jesus does not condemn her, but forgives her, calls her to a conversion of life, and enables that conversion.

When I know how much I have failed Jesus in my life, then I know how Peter must have felt when Jesus came to wash his feet. I may feel the same revulsion that Peter felt. It can be a great relief to let Jesus wash one's feet when one is aware of how sinful one is and has been. The scene in John 21 where Jesus three times asks Peter "Do you love me?" can also be a wonderfully reconciling moment for people who know that they have betrayed their best hopes and the hopes and dreams of Jesus for them.

A profound experience of the forgiveness of God and of the overwhelming realization that Jesus died for me, a sinner, leads to a great sense of freedom, a feeling that a weight has been lifted from one's soul and heart. There wells up in many people a spontaneous desire to return the favor, as it were, to get to know this Jesus who has so loved me and all human beings and suffered for me and for us. But before I take up that next stage of the Spiritual Exercises, I want to discuss in the next chapter the experience of social sin, something not so clearly present to Ignatius, but acutely present to us in this age.

Questions for prayer and/or discussion:

1. Have I ever been surprised by a new realization of my sinfulness? How did I feel and react?
2. Do I want to know how God sees me? Can I ask God to show me?
3. Are there resonances of the Spiritual Exercises in modern programs, e.g., the twelve step program of Alcoholics Anonymous?

FOOTNOTES

1. *Autobiography, op. cit.* 25.
2. *Ibid., op. cit.* 40.
3. *Ibid.,* 40.
4. *Ibid.,* 40–41.

5. "While he had these thoughts, the temptation often came over him with great force to throw himself into a large hole in his room next to the place where he was praying. But recognizing that it was a sin to kill oneself, he shouted again, 'Lord, I will do nothing to offend you'" *Ibid., op. cit.*, 35.

6. Thomas Merton, *The Seven Storey Mountain* (New York: Harcourt, Brace, 1948), pp. 206–207.

CHAPTER 4

"Show Me Your Ways": How God Reacts to the Horrors of Our World

In the previous chapter we took up the topic of asking God to reveal to us our sins and sinful tendencies. There we concentrated on the experience of individuals, as indeed does the text of *The Spiritual Exercises*. Almost twenty years ago when the retrieval of the tradition of the individual direction of the Spiritual Exercises had begun in earnest, a number of socially active Jesuits and some directors of the Exercises became concerned. They thought that this revival might lead to a kind of "me and Jesus" spirituality, a retreat from the enormous social evils our nation and world faced. To forestall such an eventuality, the Center of Concern, the Jesuit-founded center for research and advocacy for social justice, convened a task force of spiritual directors and social activists, all but one of them Jesuits. We produced the tabloid *Soundings*, a book-length series of articles on social consciousness and Ignatian spirituality.[1]

Some concepts from that task force have gained well-deserved coinage. Peter Henriot's notion of the "public dimension of the spiritual life," William Callahan's concept of "cultural addiction," and Thomas Clarke's idea of "societal grace" and "social sin" come to mind, for example. These

55

have been very helpful to me in my work as a spiritual director and writer. In my own contribution, I coined the term "social desolation" with its counterpart of "social consolation." But before I bore you with such technical details, let me give some examples.

At the end of Brian Moore's novel *Blackrobe*, the Jesuit priest Laforgue is baptizing Huron Indians knowing that their baptism will mean the end of their civilization. He has witnessed the tragic clash of alien cultures in colonial French Canada, has himself been tortured by Indians, and has at times in the novel wondered about the existence of God. The novel ends with these words: "And a prayer came to him, a true prayer at last. 'Spare them. Spare them, O Lord. Do you love us?' 'Yes.'" With these few words the novelist captures one of the deepest desires of the human heart, to know in our bones that God loves us, singly and as a whole. We want to know that God reacts favorably to us even though we feel as profoundly broken or sinful as Pére Laforgue. But how are we to know that the voice Laforgue hears or the voice we hear is actually the voice of God? Reflection on some recent experiences may help us to discern the reactions of God in our ordinary experience.

On the morning of November 16, 1989, I received a telephone call telling me of the brutal murder of six Jesuit priests, their cook, and her daughter in El Salvador. Every time I let the images of those murdered men and women touch me, I felt a sense of horror and revulsion, an involuntary turn of my head as if to ward off the sight. My blood began to boil and an almost murderous rage rose in me as I imagined the killers. Even now as I write these lines, I experience the same wave of feelings and emotions. At a memorial Mass for them I wept openly a few times, and at the end of the Mass could hardly speak my thanks to all who participated because I became so choked up with emotion.

That same Thursday I took four students at Boston College on an overnight retreat to the Jesuit house in Cohasset Harbor. We were going to spend time in private prayer to ask God to help us to experience our own and the world's creation and God's dream for us, an experience I have come to call an affective experience of Ignatius' First Principle and Foundation. Just before one of the prayer sessions I found out that my niece had given birth to her first child, a girl. With Psalm 139 as a background I began to pray. I imagined my niece and her husband holding their daughter, Cara Anne, in their arms and just marveling at the wonder of her. Suddenly I thought that this image is only a pale image of God's delight in Cara Anne and every baby born into this world. I was close to tears as I felt the welling up of a love and desire that seemed immeasurably more than my heart could hold. God's desire brings Cara Anne and every other human being into existence. How breathtakingly precious each of us is to God! I could not doubt that I was experiencing something of God's reaction to each precious life conceived on this planet.

My thoughts turned to the horrors in El Salvador that very day. Eight of God's precious children had had their lives brutally snuffed out and their bodies desecrated. How does God react to such horror? I felt again some of the same emotions I described earlier. After the centuries of human cruelty God has witnessed, I wonder whether my shock reflects God's reaction. Perhaps God still shakes his head figuratively at human inhumanity. But what about my murderous rage at the killers, my desire for vengeance? Are these emotions a reflection of God's reaction? Does God want vengeance? For some reason these emotions did not last long. I wanted the cycle of revenge and murder to stop; I did not want to have any part in continuing it. I was almost overcome again by an immense sorrow and pain and felt welling up in me almost a cry of anguish, as though God were saying: "This is not what I intend. I want all those whom I desire into life to live as

brothers and sisters, and look what they do to each other."
My rage and desire for revenge faded into the background.
The killers, for their own salvation, will have to acknowl-
edge what they have done and live with their guilt, but I
believe God does not want vengeance. "An eye for an eye"
is not God's value. I believe that I experienced something of
God's reaction to the brutality and inhumanity of human beings who, in spite of all that, are yet precious in God's eyes.
I must also add that I determined to do everything in my
power to try to get my own government to stop funding the
insane civil war in that poor country.

The outpouring of sympathy and compassion for the most
recent martyrs in El Salvador and for the poor people of that
ravaged country struck me as another indication of God's reactions to us. People are experiencing the gift of God's Holy
Spirit drawing us to compassion and solidarity with all those
who suffer. We Jesuits have been surprised at how many people of all walks of life have taken the time to write or speak
a word of sympathy and solidarity with us. One of the most
touching letters was addressed to the Jesuit community by
four students at Boston College. In part they said:

> Through our interaction with the Jesuit community at
> Boston College we have come to feel a part of the Jesuit
> family. These priests, like the Jesuits at B.C., exemplified
> their ideal of service to others through their commit-
> ment to education for faith, peace, and justice. Their
> death has left us with an ever stronger sense of their
> mission which we wish to follow. We have come to feel
> a part of the Jesuit Society and so we stand in solidarity
> with you in this time of pain.

Here, too, I sense in their words an echo of God's reaction
to this appalling situation, God drawing us together into one
family. Once again I want to underline that the reactions of
these students led them to determine to commit themselves
to the search for justice.

Finally, a few days later a woman who was deeply moved by the assassinations told me that she had had an experience of overpowering love for the people of El Salvador. Images of various faces passed before her inner eye, and she was filled with love and compassion for them and all humanity. It was almost more than her heart could bear. She was convinced that she had experienced in some pale way God's own reactions to the sufferings of human beings. She, too, has committed herself to work with the poor and downtrodden to achieve a more just society.

A few years ago in a class I was trying to get across the notion of the affective Principle and Foundation we discussed in the third chapter. I then asked the students if they had had similar experiences of a feeling of great well-being and a desire for I know not what. Most in the class nodded their heads in agreement. One woman, a nun from another continent, said that she had had such experiences, but that she had also had experiences such as the following. One evening when she returned from pastoral work in a very poor slum, she began to pray and was overcome with an enormous sadness and began to sob from the bottom of her heart. It was as if she felt deep inside her the sobbing words: "This is not the way it should be." The silence in the room was palpable. In the hush I asked her if she would want to have such experiences again. She said she would, but not as a steady diet. Her experience sounds similar to my own experience after the killing of the Jesuits and the two women. I have come to believe that such experiences give us some idea of how God reacts to the social injustices and social horrors inflicted on the majority of the people of this universe which God creates to invite all persons into the community life of the Trinity.

In Luke's gospel Jesus twice laments over Jerusalem, again giving us some inkling of God's reaction to social evil. In chapter 13 Jesus is warned to get away because Herod wants to kill him. After noting that no prophet dies outside Jerusalem, Jesus continues:

> O Jerusalem, Jerusalem, you who kill the prophets and stone those sent to you, how often I have longed to gather your children together, as a hen gathers her chicks under her wings, but you were not willing! Look, your house is left to you desolate (Lk 13:34–35).

In chapter 19 we read:

> As he approached Jerusalem and saw the city, he wept over it and said, "If you, even you, had only known on this day what would bring you peace — but now it is hidden from your eyes. The days will come upon you when your enemies will build an embankment against you and encircle you and hem you in on every side. They will dash you to the ground, you and the children within your walls. They will not leave one stone on another, because you did not recognize the time of God's coming to you" (Lk 19:41–44).

In these passages Jesus takes no pleasure in the impending destruction of Jerusalem. Rather he weeps at the hardness of heart of the people, at the social commitment or compact they seem to have made to refuse the proffered love of God. But he does not back away from his mission because of these reactions.

The very next passage in Luke gives us some sense of Jesus' rage at a social evil.

> Then he entered the temple area and began driving out those who were selling. "It is written," he said to them, "'My house will be a house of prayer,' but you have made it 'a den of robbers'" (Lk 19:45–46).

The Hebrew Bible, of course, is full of tirades by God against injustice. Jesus, in fact, in this passage is quoting Isaiah. Another example of God's reaction to social injustice is given by the prophet Amos:

This is what the Lord says:
"For three sins of Israel,
   even for four, I will not turn back my wrath.
They sell the righteous for silver,
   and the needy for a pair of sandals.
They trample on the heads of the poor
   as upon the dust of the ground
   and deny justice to the oppressed.
Father and son use the same girl
   and so profane my holy name" (Am 2:6-7).

Obviously God does not want social injustice to continue.

The examples I have given thus far are, strange to say, examples of consolation. Grief, tears of sorrow, and anger — strong anger at social injustice and at prejudice — may not seem like consolation, but in the technical sense of Ignatian spirituality they are. Ignatius writes:

> I call it consolation when an interior movement is aroused in the soul, by which it is inflamed with love of its Creator and Lord, and as a consequence, can love no creature on the face of the earth for its own sake, but only in the Creator of them all. It is likewise consolation when one sheds tears that move to the love of God, whether it be for sorrow for sins, or because of the sufferings of Christ our Lord, or for any other reason that is immediately directed to the praise and service of God. Finally, I call consolation every increase of faith, hope, and love, and all interior joy that invites and attracts to what is heavenly and to the salvation of one's soul by filling it with peace and quiet in its Creator and Lord (*Spiritual Exercises* n. 316).

In the examples I have given thus far the people felt deep compassion for suffering people and believed that they were experiencing something of God's reaction. Moreover, they felt empowered to do something to try to make the world a more just and compassionate place. They made moves to bring about community among people. I call what they experienced social consolation.

61

Perhaps my meaning will be clearer if I speak of social desolation. For Ignatius, desolation is the opposite of consolation.

> I call desolation what is entirely the opposite of (consolation), as darkness of soul, torment of spirit, inclination to what is low and earthly, restlessness rising from many disturbances and temptations which lead to want of faith, want of hope, want of love. The soul is wholly slothful, tepid, sad, and separated, as it were, from its Creator and Lord. For just as consolation is the opposite of desolation, so the thoughts that spring from consolation are the opposite of those that spring from desolation (*Spiritual Exercises* n. 317).

Personal sinfulness, addictions, and unfreedom are common sources of desolation. Experience and reflection have, however, shown that desolation can also be caused by "public" sinfulness, alienation, and unfreedom. Many people now find themselves unable to pray because they have lost hope in the institutions in which they participate.

The attitude of alienation from institutions is all-pervasive in our society. We see corruption everywhere, in government, in business, even in the church. There is a wholesale lack of trust not only of "City Hall" (meaning any institution that governs), but also of our fellow citizens. Crime on the streets is an everyday affair; people are routinely warned not to walk alone at night in certain parts of cities. Hatred often seems barely concealed and violence avoided only with great control. The point is that many of us, if not most, experience a sense of frustration and helplessness about the structures and patterns that govern our lives. We also vaguely feel some complicity in the continuance of these structures and patterns. And there are enough "do-gooders" to point the finger at us to make us feel vaguely guilty. I believe that such feelings are indications of social desolation. But like the desolation of the scrupulous person this kind of social desolation shows itself for what it really is by leading to nothing but feeling bad. It does not lead us to any positive action, to some conversion.

This is an important point. When God reveals sin to us, it is always with the purpose of moving us to amendment of life and of giving us the power to change. And only God can reveal sin. The state of sin is characterized by the inability or unwillingness to see oneself as sinner, as alienated, as part of a sinful and alienated world. Only God can break through our defences against seeing ourselves as God sees us. When we are able to look at ourselves through the eyes of the Lord who loves us into existence, only then can we see ourselves as we really are, as loved sinners in a loved and sinful world. Both the adjective and the noun in the last sentence are important. We are enabled to see ourselves as sinners in a sinful world precisely because we are loved. It is for this reason that condemnations, whether for personal or public sins, have little or no good effect unless accompanied with the message of God's abiding love.

Thus social desolation shows itself in a feeling of futility before what seem the intractable problems of our complex world. Those who find themselves in such a state, a gnawing sense of futility about the world in general and about the particular institutions to which they belong, need to be freed by the Lord just as much as an addict or habitual sinner needs to be freed by the Lord. The gnawing feeling saps life and vitality from them and keeps them from the freedom of the sons and daughters of God.

When they do let the Lord of life free them, what is the result? They feel astonished at the enormity of God's love for them and this sinful world. They feel hope for themselves and for the world. They know that in spite of all the horror, the Lord has not abandoned his people. In spite of the stupidity and evil, in spite of institutional injustice, the human spirit is not crushed and defeated. The powers of darkness have not prevailed. As a result they feel themselves empowered to try to do their part to right the social injustices in which they have participated. Gerard Manley Hopkins must have had some experiences of this powerful love of God at the heart of our sinful world to be able to write the poem "God's Grandeur" with which we will end this chapter:

> The world is charged with the grandeur of God.
>   It will flame out, like shining from shook foil;
>   It gathers to a greatness, like the ooze of oil
> Crushed. Why do men then now not reck his rod?
> Generations have trod, have trod, have trod;
>   And all is seared with trade; bleared, smeared
>   with toil;
>   And wears man's smudge and shares man's smell:
>   the soil
> Is bare now, nor can foot feel, being shod.
> And for all this, nature is never spent;
>   There lives the dearest freshness deep down
>   things;
> And though the last lights off the black West went
>   Oh, morning, at the brown brink eastward,
>   springs
> Because the Holy Ghost over the bent
>   World broods with warm breast and with ah!
>   bright wings.

Questions for prayer and/or discussion:

1.   How do I react when I read the newspapers and watch the TV news? Do I talk to God about my reactions?
2.   Do I feel that I can do little or nothing to change social structures? Can I admit this feeling to God and to others and ask their help?

FOOTNOTES

1. William R. Callahan and William A. Barry, (eds.) *Soundings: A Task Force on Social Consciousness and Ignatian Spirituality* (Washington, D.C.: Center of Concern, 1974).

CHAPTER 5

God's Dream for Our World

A dvent is a time of waiting — waiting, of course, for the
coming of Christmas, but also waiting for the second
coming of Christ. It is, however, even more a time of dream-
ing, of letting ourselves dream of great possibilities. In our
northern hemisphere it is an odd time to be letting the sap
of great desires and dreams begin to flow. After all, winter
for us is a time when everything lies fallow, when, as it were,
nature draws into itself, when little or no sap flows in the
trees. But advent goes against this grain. Often the Advent
readings speak a word of unbelievable hope to a hopeless
and exiled people. Chapter 40 of Isaiah begins what is
called Second Isaiah. The people of Israel, at least many
of them, have been carried off into exile to Babylon. The
Temple has been destroyed. The Israelite's plight and their
sense of hopelessness can be heard in the following words of
Psalm 137:

> By the rivers of Babylon we sat and wept
>   when we remembered Zion.
> There on the poplars we hung our harps,
> for there our captors asked us for songs,
>   our tormentors demanded songs of joy;
> they said, "Sing us one of the songs of Zion!"
> How can we sing the songs of the Lord
>   while in a foreign land? (Ps 137:1–4).

66

To a people feeling so hopeless and bereft — and so sinful — the word of the Lord comes through the mouth of Second Isaiah:

> Comfort, comfort my people,
> says your God.
> Speak tenderly to Jerusalem, and proclaim to her
> that her hard service has been completed,
> that her sin has been paid for (Is 40:1–2).

Even as we hear these words, many of us recall the opening song of Handel's *Messiah,* the promise of Second Isaiah that the Lord would make a highway through the desert, fill every valley, and make every mountain and hill low so that the exiled people could return to their beloved Zion and live in peace.

Such Old Testament prophecies touch us directly too, don't they? They speak to something deep in us that yearns for a world of peace and prosperity and harmony. We thrill to the dream of a time when swords will be beaten into plowshares, when wars will be no more, when people will neither harm nor destroy on all God's holy mountain, when the wolf will lie down with the lamb, when all men and women will live as brothers and sisters. I believe that we are in touch with God's dream for the universe when we allow ourselves, almost despite ourselves, to thrill to these prophecies, when we allow them to awaken in us the desires for a world so different from the one we actually inhabit. And Christians believe that Jesus Christ is the fulfillment of these prophecies, that he wants to lead us into the promised land and can do it if we follow him.

In a similar context I recalled Martin Luther King's electrifying "I Have a Dream" speech in September, 1963, at the tremendous gathering for the civil rights of Afro-Americans in Washington, D.C. Just as his refrain "I have a dream . . ." "I have a dream . . ." "I have a dream . . ." "I have a dream . . ." sends a thrill through those who hear or read

that speech, so too the Advent readings send a thrill of desire and hope through us.[1]

Again in the same prophecy from Second Isaiah we hear
words that have become one of the more popular of the
songs of the St. Louis Jesuits: "Like a shepherd he feeds his
flock, and gathers the lambs in his arms, holding them carefully close to his heart, leading them home." Such a beautiful
image of a tender God taking care of his troubled and bereft
people. The early Christians felt that Jesus was the fulfillment
of that image. John's gospel has Jesus say:

> "I am the good shepherd. The good shepherd lays down
> his life for the sheep. . . . I am the good shepherd. I
> know my sheep and my sheep know me — just as the
> Father knows me and I know the Father — and I lay
> down my life for the sheep. I have other sheep that are
> not of this sheep pen. I must bring them also. They too
> will listen to my voice, and there shall be one flock and
> one shepherd" (Jn 10:11, 14-16).

What we are beginning to notice here is that the Old
Testament prophecies evoked a dream in the people who
first heard them, gave them hope, and enabled them to carry
on in difficult circumstances. The early Christians had the
same dreams evoked by these prophecies, but they felt something wholly different. Their experience of the risen Jesus
told them that the dream, the hope, the desire was already
fulfilled. Jesus is the fulfillment of our wildest dreams. Jesus
is the liberator of desire, as Sebastian Moore describes him.[2]
In the risen Jesus we meet our deepest desire personified. It is
almost too much to believe — and, in fact, most of us do not
fully believe it. Otherwise we would not lead such humdrum,
mediocre, sort of dragging lives. But occasionally the dream
takes hold and we feel more alive, less afraid of life and the
future, and we have some inkling of the incredible beauty
and mystery of our lives and of our universe. Let me recall

68

again Pearl Tull's words in her diary as portrayed in Anne Tyler's novel, *Dinner at the Homesick Restaurant.*

> "Early this morning. . . I went out behind the house to weed. Was kneeling in the dirt by the stable with my pinafore a mess and perspiration rolling down my back, wiped my face on my sleeve, reached for the trowel, and all at once thought, Why I believe that at just this moment I am absolutely happy. . . .
>
> "The Bedloe girl's piano scales were floating out her window. . . and a bottle fly was buzzing in the grass, and I saw that I was kneeling on such a beautiful green little planet. I don't care what else might come about, I have had this moment. It belongs to me."[3]

Another Advent prophecy comes from the book of Jeremiah.

> "The days are coming," declares the Lord, "when I will fulfill the gracious promise I made to the house of Israel and to the house of Judah.
>
> > "In those days and at that time,
> > I will make a righteous Branch sprout from
> >   David's line;
> >   he will do what is just and right in the land.
> >   In those days Judah will be saved
> > and Jerusalem will live in safety.
> > This is the name by which it will be called:
> > The Lord Our Righteousness" (Jer 33:14–16).

Notice the dream of a prosperous and safe time. Once again, the early Christians pointed to the risen Jesus and said: "Here this prophecy is fulfilled in our eyes."

The prophet who is called Third Isaiah proclaims his mission in these words:

> The Spirit of the Sovereign Lord is on me,
>   because the Lord has anointed me
>   to preach good news to the poor.
> He has sent me to bind up the brokenhearted,
>   to proclaim freedom for the captives
>   and release from darkness for the prisoners,

to proclaim the year of the Lord's favor
and the day of vengeance of our God,
to comfort all who mourn (Is 61:1–2).

In Luke's gospel Jesus reads these words in the synagogue
and then announces that they have been fulfilled in their
hearing. Once again we see a dream described and then the
affirmation that Jesus is the fulfillment of the dream (Lk
4:14–21).

Deep within us, I believe, God's dream draws us toward
this desire of the everlasting hills. God creates a universe
in which God continually attracts us into communion and
community with God, the perfect community of Father,
Word, and Spirit. God's Spirit dwelling in our hearts pushes
that dream of God toward our consciousness. That dream
is touched by the myths of the Holy Grail, by the stories of
Camelot and King Arthur, by the myths created by J.R.R.
Tolkien in his trilogy *The Lord of the Rings*, and perhaps even
by Western movies and cheap romances. Tolkien himself
seems to indicate this.

> The consolation of fairy-stories, the joy of the happy
> ending . . . is a sudden and miraculous grace . . . . It
> does not deny the existence . . . of sorrow and failure:
> the possibility of these is necessary to the joy of deliv-
> erance; it denies (in the face of much evidence, if you
> will) universal defeat and in so far is *evangelium*, giving
> a fleeting glimpse of Joy, Joy beyond the walls of the
> world, poignant as grief.
>
> It is the mark of a good fairy-story, of the higher
> or more complete kind, that however wild its events,
> however fantastic or terrible the adventures, it can give
> to child or man that hears it, when the "turn" comes, a
> catch of the breath, a beat and lifting of the heart, near
> to (or indeed accompanied by) tears, as keen as that
> given by any form of literary art, and having a peculiar
> quality.[4]

In the Spiritual Exercises Ignatius introduces a consideration of the call of an earthly king as a prelude to the contemplation of the life of Christ. I believe that his parable of an earthly king is such a fairy-story, aimed at eliciting that same deep desire that is aroused by the prophecies of the Hebrew Bible and the myths we have just been speaking about.[5] Ignatius was a reformed soldier, you recall, and a fiery, brave, and fiercely loyal one at that. So he introduces a consideration of a king with all the virtues of a Christian king, but a king who has never existed in reality. Hence, in a real sense, it is a fairy-story. In Ignatius' day the great threat to Christian Europe were the "infidels" at the gates. So this great king invites all people of good will to labor with him, share his sufferings and hunger and pains in order to share with him the victory that was assured. Many of us have trouble with the military images. They are not, however, in my estimation, the real point. The real point is that deep in all our hearts is the desire for a universe where all men and women are united in one family under God. Ignatius' parable wants to arouse that desire in us and then point to Jesus as the one who will lead us to the fulfillment of that deepest desire of our hearts.

There are moments when we can almost taste the desire for a world such as God promises in the prophecies of the Hebrew Bible. But too often we stifle the desire, the dream. The voice of reason tells us that such dreams are pipe dreams, not attainable in the real world in which we live. Sebastian Moore calls this voice of reason the voice of original sin, a voice whose siren call is that nothing will ever change for the better.

> Sin, then, is a deep-seated reluctance to grow, to change, to open the mind, to respond to the promptings of the Holy Spirit. So it is a tendency to block the insight that would show me that I am painting myself into a corner needlessly. "Needlessly?" I ask

when the insight tries to get through. "No, I've got to
do it this way, it's always done this way, there is no
other way." That's the voice of sin.[6]

That we so easily believe this siren voice within us is a mystery. We do have experiences not only of having the dream
evoked within us and of feeling more free and more whole,
but also of feeling that others feel the same way. In other
words, we experience that we are not alone. Yet we still listen to the siren call. In a number of articles I have explored
a very strange resistance to developing a closer relationship
with God. The strangeness is that the resistance seems to
come on strongly after very positive experiences of God.[7]
The awakening of the deep desire for a world such as the
prophets of the Hebrew Bible evoke in us is such a positive
experience, the Joy Tolkien mentions. Yet we pass it off as
though it were just a hopeless pipe dream. There is in us a
deep-seated reluctance to believe in our deepest desires.

Yet Ignatius wants to have us believe in the dream of
God and to realize that God wants us to be a part of his
dream for our world. That's right. After using the parable
or myth to help the dream to come to the surface, Ignatius
then tells the retreatant to look at Jesus as the fulfillment of
the dream. Tetlow translates or paraphrases the second part
of this kingdom meditation in this way.

> If a charismatic secular leader could demand loyalty (and
> many less excellent ones get unquestioning loyalty from
> their friends), what about Jesus Christ, whom God has
> made eternal King?
> I let my fancy roam. I imagine Jesus surrounded by
> seventy-two disciples. They sit on a hill. Jesus talks with
> them, saying something like this: "It is my will to win
> over the whole of humankind. No enemy can defeat
> me or finally interfere with my kingdom. I will draw all
> to myself. I will stay with my friends and we will labor
> and struggle, watch and pray. No one will have to go
> through anything that I do not myself go through.

Whoever works with me and suffers with me will also
share the glory of the kingdom with me. I assure you,
I will see my project crowned with total success." After
feeling how wonderfully attractive Jesus' invitation is,
gently end the fantasy.

Then consider that anyone with any sense at all will
follow Jesus Christ. Consider this: some might want to
walk more closely with Jesus Christ in this enterprise,
though they cannot explain their desiring. If you feel in-
clined to do so, formally say this prayer to Jesus Christ:

Before we read that prayer, I want to underline the fact
that Ignatius is speaking of a desiring that comes up in a person. He is not speaking of an obligation, a "should." The way
Tetlow puts it, the person may not even be able to explain
the desiring. Now here is the prayer:

Eternal Lord of all things,
I feel Your gaze on me.
I sense that your mother stands near, watching,
and that with you are all the great beings of
    heaven —
angels and powers and martyrs and saints.
Lord, Jesus, I think you have put a desire in me.
If you will help me, please,
I would like to make my offering:
I want it to be my desire, and my choice,
provided that you want it, too,
to live my life as you lived yours.
I know that you lived as an insignificant person
in a little, despised town;
I know that you rarely tasted luxury and never,
    privilege,
and that you resolutely refused to accept power.
I know that you suffered rejection by leaders,
abandonment by friends, and failure.
I know. I can hardly bear the thought of it all.
But it seems a toweringly wonderful thing
that you might call me to follow you and stand
    with you.

I will labor with you to bring God's reign,
if you will give me the gift to do it. Amen.[8]

The retreatant who can say this prayer with honesty is
not at this time making a decision about his or her way of
life. The retreatant is voicing a desire, a desire believed to
have been evoked by Jesus himself. But he or she could be
wrong about the origin of the desire, and so says: "I want it
to be my desire, and my choice, *provided that you want it, too,*
to live my life as you lived yours." It may well be, in other
words, that during the further days of the retreat and because
of the realities of life, the retreatant will discover that he
or she is not called to live precisely as Jesus lived. The retreatant further says: "But it seems a toweringly wonderful
thing that you might call me to follow you and stand with
you." Again we note the tentativeness of the response. "Yes, I
am deeply attracted to following you; it sends a thrill through
me, but I want to be sure that you are calling me to this."
And finally he or she says: "I will labor with you to bring
God's reign, *if you will give me the gift to do it.*" At this point
in the retreat Ignatius does not want the retreatant to make
any rash promises or to think that the work of the retreat
is over.

Retreatants who at this point have the desire we have
been discussing want to get to know Jesus better in order
to love him more and to follow him more closely. This desire, Ignatius expects, will carry the person through the next
part of the retreat, which is called the Second Week. (But
remember that a "week" in the Exercises has nothing to
do with the number of days.) What the retreatant wants is
that Jesus reveal himself, his values, his dreams, his loves,
and his hates so that the retreatant will actually love him
as a true friend and leader and become more like him. Retreatants, at this stage, are asking whether they can and may
make Jesus and the mission of Jesus the center around which
they will organize their lives. In the history of the Spiritual

Exercises this question has been considered to be a question of whether the person had a "call" to live a vowed life in a congregation. I want to reflect with you for a few moments on this subject.

In an illuminating chapter of *New Wineskins* Sandra Schneiders contrasts the "religious" person with the artist and the intellectual. Just as the artist organizes his or her life around the aesthetic dimension of experience and the intellectual around the life of the mind, so the religious person organizes his or her life around the religious dimension of experience.

> Such a person is not necessarily the most religiously talented (although some natural bent toward and taste for religious experience is undoubtedly at work), the holiest, or the most virtuous. But religion, the horizon of ultimacy, the quest for the Transcendent, exercises a fascination in the life of this person that relativizes all the "normal" concerns of human life.[9]

Jesus was "religious" in this sense. His prime concern was God and God's reign. The disciples of Jesus were also "religious" in this sense. But I do not believe that one has to take the vows of the "religious life" in order to be religious in this sense. I have met and directed many people who have felt the call to organize their lives around the love of Jesus and his mission without feeling any need to join a religious congregation.

Let me sum up. God is always creating a universe in which God draws all persons into the community of the Trinity. This "drawing" is God's dream and is experienced by us as the desire for the fulfillment of the dreams of the prophecies read in Advent. Christians believe that Jesus in his mission to announce the coming reign of God is the fulfillment in the flesh of this desire. Ignatius tries to help those who want to pay attention to that desire to let it unfold and become centered on Jesus.

Questions for prayer and/or discussion:

1. Have I felt or do I feel the deep desire to live in union with God and in harmony with all people and all creation? Do I want to talk to God and others about this desire?
2. How did I react when I read the prayer, "Eternal Lord of all things"?

FOOTNOTES

1. See William A. Barry, *Paying Attention to God: Discernment in Prayer* (Notre Dame, IN: Ave Maria Press, 1990), pp. 55–62.

2. Sebastian Moore, *Jesus the Liberator of Desire* (New York: Crossroad, 1989).

3. Anne Tyler, *Dinner at the Homesick Restaurant* (New York: Berkley Books, 1983), p. 284.

4. J. R. R. Tolkien, *The Tolkien Reader* (New York: Ballantine), pp. 68–69.

5. See William J. Connolly, "Story of the Pilgrim King and the Dynamics of Prayer," *Review for Religious*, 32, 1973, pp. 268–272. Also in David L. Fleming (ed.), *Notes on the Spiritual Exercises of St. Ignatius of Loyola* (St. Louis, MO: Review for Religious, 1983, 103–1–7).

6. Sebastian Moore, *Let This Mind Be in You: The Quest for Identity Through Oedipus to Christ* (Minneapolis, Chicago, New York: Winston, 1985), p. 85.

7. Three of these articles are reprinted in *Paying Attention to God: Discernment in Prayer, op. cit.*, pp. 31–51.

8. Joseph A. Tetlow, *Choosing Christ in the World, op. cit.*, pp. 148–149.

9. Sandra Schneiders, *New Wineskins: Re-imagining Religious Life Today* (New York/Mahwah: Paulist Press, 1986), pp. 34–35.

CHAPTER 6

Ignatian Contemplation of the Gospels

L et's start very far from the topic of this chapter. One of the great geniuses of this century is Sigmund Freud. Have you ever wondered what his core insight was? I believe that the original insight from which most of the rest of Freud's work stemmed was the realization that people's most bizarre and irrational behavior, thoughts, and symptoms are meaningful. In other words, for Freud, neurotic and psychotic symptoms and thoughts and behaviors have a psychological meaning, make sense, even though they seem totally nonsensical. Thus Freud tried to discover the psychological meaning of dreams, slips of the tongue and pen, momentary forgetting, and jokes. Basically he assumed that every human experience and behavior could be explained in psychological terms; it had, therefore, a psychological dimension.

Now we come closer to our topic. What was the original insight of Ignatius of Loyola? I would say it was the idea that God can be found in all things, that every human experience has a religious dimension or meaning. The point is illustrated in the story of Ignatius' conversion which we related in the first chapter. You recall that the convalescing Ignatius engaged in two sets of daydreams, one of knightly deeds to win the favor of a high-born lady, the

other of following Christ as did the saints. Eventually
Ignatius realized that God was using his imagination, his
daydreaming, to draw him to God's service. If God can be
found in daydreams, then God can be found in every human
experience.

Indeed, in the previous chapter, we spoke of how the
myth of the hero speaks to us of God's dream for our world
and that in Jesus that myth finds its fulfillment. Ignatius encourages retreatants to imagine a great secular leader, for him
a king who is a military leader, who calls all people of good
will to follow him in battles and sufferings to certain victory over the "infidels." Then they let the image of Jesus help
them to realize that the desires aroused by the imaginary king
are fulfilled in Jesus. It was probably the insight he gained
from his daydreams during convalescence that provided the
kernel of the kingdom meditation which is placed at the
beginning of that part of the Spiritual Exercises given over
to contemplating the public life of Jesus. It is aimed to fire
the imagination with desire to know Jesus better in order to
love him more and to follow him more closely. Ignatius also
learned through his own long period of conversion at Manresa that God uses the gospel stories to draw us imaginatively
into their world in order to let Jesus reveal himself to us. So
let us look at some of the suggestions Ignatius makes in the
Exercises.

After the kingdom meditation Ignatius proposes that the
next day be taken up with contemplation of two mysteries,
the Incarnation and the Nativity, and then with two repetitions of these contemplations, and finally with what he
calls the application of the interior senses to the material
contemplated during the day. Ignatius develops these two
contemplations at length to exemplify a typical day of prayer
in this period of the Exercises. After this his comments are
quite sparse.

Each period of contemplation begins with the usual preparatory prayer of recalling the presence of God and asking that all one's intentions, actions, and operations be directed to the praise and service of God. Then one reads the text of scripture. Actually, since texts of scripture were not very plentiful in Ignatius' time, he speaks of recalling the history of the mystery of the Incarnation. After the text is read, he asks the retreatant to imagine the place. In the instance of the Incarnation, he first suggests imagining the whole world and then focusing on the village of Nazareth and the house of Mary. The third prelude is to ask for what I want and desire during this period of prayer, and in this instance and throughout this period of the Exercises the desire of the retreatant is "to ask for an intimate knowledge of our Lord, who has become human for me, that I may love him more and follow more closely" (*Spiritual Exercises* n. 104). In the previous chapter I mentioned that this desire is a desire for a personal revelation of Jesus to me about his values, his hopes and dreams, his loves and hates. We do not love an abstraction, but a person whom we know well and intimately. In John's gospel during the last discourse Jesus says to his disciples,

> I no longer call you servants, because a servant does not know his master's business. Instead, I have called you friends, for everything I have learned from my Father I have made known to you (Jn 15:15).

The desire of the Ignatian retreatant takes Jesus at his word.

Then Ignatius asks the retreatant to use his or her imagination. The text of Luke's gospel begins:

> In the sixth month, God sent the angel Gabriel to Nazareth, a town in Galilee, to a virgin pledged to be married to a man named Joseph, a descendant of David. The virgin's name was Mary. The angel went to her and said, "Greetings, you who are highly favored! The Lord is with you" (Lk 1:26–28).

79

Here is how Ignatius' own imagination must have worked with this text. The text says that God sent the angel. So Ignatius imagines the Trinity looking down at the world they are creating. What do they see? They see all the people of the world, some white, some black, some yellow, some red, some rich, some poor, some at peace, some at war, some laughing, some sorrowful, some healthy, some sick, etc. What do the persons of the Trinity hear among all these people? What do they see all these people doing to one another? Do you see what Ignatius is suggesting? He suggests that we ask God to reveal to us through our imaginations how God views the world. What would have led God to decide to send the angel to Mary and to send the Second Person of the Trinity to become a fetus in her womb?

Here we might recall what we said when we asked about God's reactions to the horrors of our world. Sometimes we experience a terrible sadness and anger as we read the newspapers or watch the news on TV, when we recall the horrors of the concentration camps and the Holocaust of Nazi Germany, when we read of the torture and murder of innocent people, when we hear of the brutal treatment of children. It can be as though we feel, deep within us, an enormous sob that seems much larger than anything we could hold that says: "This is not what we intended with this world." Ignatius is encouraging such a use of imagination here.

Then he asks us to imagine the response of the Trinity. Are they enraged? Do they decide to destroy the world because so few people even try to live as brothers and sisters. No! They decide to send the Second Person to become human. Moreover, they decide to take a tremendous risk. The angel Gabriel will not command Mary to become the mother of God; he will ask her. Imagine the condescension of God.

And so after we have imagined the Trinity's contemplation of the world and their decision, the scene shifts to a small, backward town. Remember Nathaniel's words when he is first told of Jesus of Nazareth. "Nazareth! Can anything good come from there?" (Jn 1:46). My recollection from Ricciotti's *Life Of Christ* is that Nazareth in Jesus' time was a village where many of the homes were little more than caves. And Mary is believed to have been little more than a young girl. The imagination seems to go from the sublime to the ridiculous.

Ignatius asks us to imagine the scene as the angel approaches Mary, to notice them and what they say and do. The previous scene in heaven has, perhaps, prepared us for the drama of this one. How would you feel if such a strange experience occurred to you? Wouldn't you be afraid? Would you think you were going crazy? In a real sense God's plan for the universe depends on this encounter, on the response of this little slip of a girl. Can we feel the tension, perhaps the hope, that she will say yes? Would I say yes to such a request of God to me? Would I want to be able to say yes, even if I was scared of the consequences? Does it run through Mary's mind what the neighbors and Joseph will think when they find out that she is pregnant? One can also imagine the risk God takes in sending the Second Person of the Trinity to become a fetus, how tiny and frail the vessel of our salvation is at this point in time. These are only suggestions from my own imagination. Each one of us will imagine the scene in a different way as we ponder the text of Luke and the mystery of God's action in this world.

Ignatius suggests that we finish with what he calls a colloquy, a conversation with the persons we have met in the contemplation. What do I want to say to the Persons of the Trinity, to Mary, to Jesus? He ends: "According to the light that I have received, I will beg for grace to follow and imitate our Lord, who has just become human for me. Close with an Our Father" (*Spiritual Exercises* n. 109). Notice that Ignatius expects that this kind of contemplation will make the mystery present to me now. That's the purpose of these contemplations, to make present the revelation of the Lord to me in my life.

The second contemplation, that of the mystery of the birth of Christ, begins with the same introductory prayer and the same three preludes to reading the text, imagining the place, and expressing my desire to know Jesus more intimately in order to love him more and to follow him more closely. Then in the contemplation proper Ignatius again suggests we use our imaginations to see the persons, hear what they are saying to one another, and what they are doing. In this one he suggests the following: "I will make myself a poor little unworthy slave, and as though present, look upon them, contemplate them, and serve them in their needs with all possible homage and reverence" (*Spiritual Exercises* n. 114). I have known women who have helped Mary with the delivery in their contemplation. One pediatrician whom I directed was thrilled that he could help Mary through the time of labor just as he had helped so many women. Both men and women have imagined themselves holding the newborn Jesus as they have held infants of their own or of relatives or friends. Ignatius' suggestion from his own imagination of becoming a humble slave gives us the freedom to let our own imagination take us into this scene of great mystery and the risk of God. Our imagination lets us realize how fragile God's hopes for the universe are when they rest on a newborn infant. Again, Ignatius' own imagination has him imagining the persons "making the journey and laboring that our Lord might be born in extreme poverty, and that after many labors, after hunger, thirst, heat, cold, after insults and outrages, he might die on the cross, and all this for me" (*Spiritual Exercises* n. 116).

This kind of contemplation or use of the imagination can be done in any number of ways. Tetlow suggests the following:

Then I enter the event. I can do that in many different ways, and nothing constrains me to do it one way rather than another.

— One way that helps some people: I notice the people themselves, keenly, lovingly. Then I listen to what they say. Then I watch how they are acting.

— Another way that helps: I simply get involved in the event, at whatever point I feel drawn into it. I act in it, a part of the event — holding the light, fixing the hayrack, helping the animals.

— And a final way: I go along with one of the persons in the event, letting the event be a dynamic background. We talk with and listen to one another.[1]

The point is that we are asked to trust that the Holy Spirit of God who dwells in our hearts will use our imaginations in order to reveal to us who Jesus is.

When I talk about imagination in prayer in this way, it often happens that people think that it's not for them. They think that I am talking about a kind of imagination that can create a movie inside their heads. There are people, of course, who have such imaginations, and I have often envied them their ability to produce such interesting stories. But I believe that each of us has an imagination. Only we have different kinds of imaginations. For example, I say, and believe, that Jesus is my companion and leader. I stake my life on my commitment to him. But I have no idea what he looks like. Yet I sense how he feels at times and have had some idea of how he feels about me. For many years as a Jesuit I thought that I was somehow deficient in my prayer life because I could never produce a picture of Jesus. I have come to realize that each of us has a different way of imagining. If you can read a novel and get involved in the characters, then you have an imagination. If you can be moved by a play or by music or by a painting, you have an imagination. If you can weep for someone who tells you about the loss of a loved one, you have an imagination. As I put it once, if you can wince when someone tells you about hitting his thumb with a hammer, you have an imagination. "Imaginations differ; we need to let God use the one we have and not bemoan the one we do not have."[2]

A key Ignatian concept about prayer is the idea of savoring what one has received. Our tendency would be to race on to new and better insights and experiences. But Ignatius puts the brakes on. Here in the beginning of the stage of getting to know Jesus better he suggests two new contemplations each day with two repetitions followed at the end of the day with what is called an application of the senses. During the repetitions Ignatius suggests that we go back to savor those aspects of the previous contemplations that gave us more consolation, but also to return to the points that might have troubled us. Thus, someone who was deeply consoled by the image of holding the newborn Jesus could go back to that image and see if the Lord is communicating even more than what at first blush he or she thought. Ignatius, the shrewd spiritual director and psychologist, realizes that we can too easily pass over very deep consolations and miss their real point for us. I have known people, for example, who have realized that they very quickly forget the good things that happen to them only to concentrate on the negatives. By the same token, Ignatius suggests that people return to those points of the contemplations that were especially difficult or painful. For example, a woman who had a very troublesome experience with the nativity scene found upon returning to it more than once that her own childlessness was a source of great anguish and anger at God. Because it is so easy to deceive oneself, it is good to have a spiritual director to whom one can tell the truth of what actually happened in order to begin to discern what God is communicating.

This last comment leads us to the question of discernment of spirits. When we pray — no matter what method we use — there are many influences at work. Every human

84

experience has a physiological dimension because we are people with bodies and digestive and eliminative processes. A
good or bad night's sleep, for example, can affect our contemplation. Every human experience has a psychological
dimension because we approach any new experience with
all the psychological baggage we carry from our past experience with significant people. Thus, our experience of God or
of Jesus will be affected by our past experience with significant people in our lives as well as by our past learning about
God and Jesus. Just imagine how the experience of God as
Father is influenced by an experience of having been abused
physically and sexually by one's own father.

Every human experience also has a sociological and cultural dimension because we are influenced by the society and
culture we grew up in. Because of their cultural upbringing
Jews experience God differently than Roman Catholics do.
Moreover, the history of spirituality tells us that God's Holy
Spirit is not the only spirit at work in our world. In fact,
Ignatian spirituality is predicated on the fact that the evil
spirit is also at work trying to draw us away from the ways
of God. With all these influences we need to engage in the
discernment of spirits to discover what is of God in our experiences. Ignatius gives us some guidelines in the Spiritual
Exercises.

The most important guidelines are contained in the very
first rules for the discernment of spirits. There Ignatius says
that for those who are going from one mortal sin to another
— that is, for those who are living lives out of tune with
God's intention for this world — the action of the evil spirit
is to "propose apparent pleasures. He fills their imagination
with sensual delights and gratifications. . ." (*Spiritual Exercises* n. 314). Just think of times when you were tempted to
live a lie and you will know what Ignatius means. He then
goes on to note that with such persons "the good spirit uses a
method which is the reverse of the above. Making use of the

light of reason, he will rouse the sting of conscience and fill them with remorse" (*Spiritual Exercises* n. 314). Again think of how ill at ease we feel when we have done something that is hurtful to someone. I still feel in my bones remorse about a spiteful and hurting remark I made, with full consciousness, about a grammar school classmate.

On the other hand, Ignatius speaks of those who are trying to live in tune with God's intentions for this world. With these people "it is characteristic of the evil spirit to harass with anxiety, to afflict with sadness, to raise obstacles backed by fallacious reasonings that disturb the soul. Thus he seeks to prevent the soul from advancing" (*Spiritual Exercises* n. 315). Ignatius himself gives a good example in his autobiography: "A harsh thought came to trouble him by pointing out the hardship of his life, as if someone was saying within his soul, 'How will you be able to endure this life for the seventy years you have yet to live?'"[3] Ignatius recognized that he could not guarantee himself even one more day of life. Many of those who have accepted the way of life of Alcoholics Anonymous will recognize this temptation. On the other hand, for such people who are trying to live good, Christian lives "it is characteristic of the good spirit . . . to give courage and strength, consolations, tears, inspirations, and peace" (*Spiritual Exercises* n. 315).

In other words, if our general orientation is toward trying to align ourselves with the intentions of God, then we can discern that an experience is of God if it leads us forward, gives us hope and élan, moves us toward freedom, indeed, helps us to move at all. The effects of the evil spirit and of our own resistance are to keep us in a rut, asking unanswerable questions, leading us nowhere but to ennui and despair. Thus, if our use of the imagination in prayer leads us to more trust in life, to more hope for the future, and to more love of Jesus, then we can be sure that we are on the right track.

For the final contemplation of the day Ignatius suggests that the person use all his or her imaginative senses to go back over all that has been contemplated during the day. It is one further way to deepen the experience of the presence of the mysteries of the Lord's life to the retreatant. This period of prayer is intended to be a savoring of the whole day, a way of letting the revelation of Jesus sink into the depths of our hearts.

Questions for prayer and/or discussion:

1. What kind of imagination do I have? How does God's self-revelation come to me?
2. How do I answer Jesus' question, "Who do *you* say I am?" Can I tell him who he is for me?

FOOTNOTES

1. Joseph A. Tetlow, *Choosing Christ in the World, op. cit.*, p. 155.

2. William A. Barry, *God and You: Prayer as a Personal Relationship* (New York/Mahwah: Paulist Press, 1987), p. 42.

3. *Autobiography of Ignatius of Loyola, op. cit.*, pp. 33–34.

CHAPTER 7

Letting Jesus Reveal
Himself to Me

In the previous chapter we spoke of Ignatian contemplation, the use of one's imagination to let Jesus reveal himself to us so that we may love him more and follow him
more closely. Once again I want to emphasize that Ignatius
does not tell people what to desire. Ignatius hopes that if
they allow God to lead them as God led him, their deepest
desires will gradually emerge. Moreover their desires will also
change in the course of the developing relationship with the
Mystery we call God, Father, Son, and Holy Spirit. Ignatius
expects that the relationship itself with God will not only
change and develop our minds but also affect our hearts, our
desires, our hopes.

Ignatius notes of himself that "God treated him at this
time just as a schoolmaster treats a child whom he is teaching."[1] But he then goes on to note that God had given him a
strong desire to serve God. Gradually, through the experience
of his developing relationship with God, his desires were pu-
rified and channeled. The ambitious and fiery knight who
wanted to do the same or even greater deeds of asceticism
as St. Francis or St. Dominic now could frame his desires
in the passionate, yet humble way he voices the offering of
the kingdom meditation: "I want it to be my desire, and my

88

choice, *provided that you want it, too,* to live my life as you lived yours."[2]

I bring this up once again to underscore the notion that the desire to know Jesus in order to love him more and to follow him more closely has to be a real one, not a "should." For example, just because I am in the tenth day of my thirty-day retreat, I *should* desire to know Jesus better, even though, in fact, I really want to know that he forgives me. Often enough directors of the Exercises have to remind retreatants that they can only desire what they really do desire. Desires are not under our control. If we do not like some of our desires, we can ask God to help us to overcome them or to change them. Also if people do not desire something which they want to desire, they can ask God to help them to desire it, to attract them to this desire. People are often helped a great deal if they know that they can tell God the real truth about their desires. For example, people can tell Jesus that they do not feel very attracted to him, but would like to be. This is first-class prayer.

But let's get back to the persons who do desire to know Jesus better so as to love him more and to follow him more closely. In the previous chapter we spoke of the first day of what Ignatius calls the Second Week of the Exercises in which retreatants contemplate the Incarnation and the Nativity of Jesus with the repetitions as we mentioned. After going into such great detail in the two contemplations in order to indicate the method, Ignatius becomes laconic, merely giving indications of the texts of the gospels to be contemplated. Different directors go about the subsequent contemplations of the public life of Jesus in different ways. I have a tendency to recommend Mark's gospel unless the retreatant has another preference. I look at Mark's gospel as almost a paradigm of how Jesus develops his relationship with his disciples. The gospel, thus, allows Jesus to reveal himself to the retreatant and allows the retreatant to react to Jesus and his values, life, and call. I propose to take us through some of the early chapters of Mark to indicate how we might approach letting Jesus reveal himself to us.

During a retreat I ask the retreatant to spend one period of prayer reading the first ten chapters of Mark. It usually takes about forty-five to fifty minutes. People rarely read a whole gospel in one sitting like this. Thus it is a novel experience and can even give a person a better sense of how the gospel is a unity, not just disparate scenes. The first ten chapters cover the public life of Jesus up to the beginning of the last week of his life.

Different people note different aspects of Jesus in such a period of prayer. Some note that he is a man of great purpose and energy. Some focus on his compassion to those in need. Some feel his passion and the intensity of his love for his Father and his Father's business. Some dwell on how often he takes time out to pray. Once a group of Jesuits had spent an hour reading the first ten chapters in this way and then shared their impressions. It amazed us how differently we experienced Jesus. One man, a social activist, later told me that he did not believe the people who noticed the number of times Jesus went off by himself to pray until he went back to reread the gospel. He then realized that he had been neglecting prayer in his own life and did not want to see that Jesus took time to pray.

These different reactions to the reading of the gospel can come from two sources. The last example shows us the possibility that our own blind spots can get in the way of seeing Jesus as he really is in the gospel. Also we can see in Jesus what we want to see to confirm our own image of ourselves. I recall one man who saw only the kindness of Jesus and did not notice until it was pointed out to him that Jesus is often angry in Mark's gospel. In his own life he did not know how to deal with his own anger and, indeed, repressed it. These last examples illustrate a selective contemplation of the gospel. We must also remember, however, that we have asked Jesus to reveal himself to us through this reading of the gospel. Thus, we must expect that some of what we notice and focus on will be a personal revelation of Jesus to us. Sometimes he will reveal one aspect of himself because that is what we need at that time, at other times another aspect. This is one of the ways in which God does communicate with us. Ignatian contemplation takes very seriously that the relationship is a two-way street.

After retreatants have spent one period reading the gospel, I then encourage them to use the other periods of prayer of that day to go over those scenes that made the strongest impact on them. Some of the reactions may be negative. For example, a man could get angry because Jesus seems so much in a hurry. He could go back to talk over with Jesus this reaction and see how Jesus responds. A woman might get angry because he picks only men as apostles. She might take up this reaction with Jesus. Whatever makes a strong impact on us can become grist for the mill of our continuing relationship with Jesus.

After one day spent on the whole of the public life in Mark, we can begin to look in more detail at the gospel, always with the desire that Jesus reveal himself personally to me in order that I may love him more and follow him more closely. Here, I want to indicate ways of contemplating some of these earlier chapters of Mark's gospel.

Near the beginning of the gospel Jesus appeared before John the baptizer, this wild man, who had been whetting the people's appetite for the messiah, very clearly indicating that he himself was not the one.

> At that time Jesus came from Nazareth in Galilee and was baptized by John in the Jordan. As Jesus was coming up out of the water, he saw heaven being torn open and the Spirit descending on him like a dove. And a voice

91

came from heaven: "You are my Son, whom I love; with
you I am well pleased" (Mk 1:9–11).

We try to imagine that scene and let Jesus reveal to us whatever he wants to reveal. But we may have some questions
for him. "What was it like to meet John? Did you like him?"
"How did you react to the crowds and to the publicity of
this act?" "How did you feel when you heard the voice from
heaven?" People have felt delighted for Jesus that he was
so affirmed by his Father, and they have somehow also felt
that God was happy that they wanted to come closer to his
beloved Son. Some have felt that God was also pleased with
them and linked them with Jesus. In this way they experienced in a new and much more heartfelt way what it means
to be another Christ. Some, too, have found that they were
frightened by the closeness of the Mystery we call God to
Jesus and to themselves. Some have recoiled in a strange way
from the very intimacy they thought they desired. Again we
see that the different reactions can become part of the ongoing dialogue with Jesus that such contemplation seeks to
foster.

After a short indication that Jesus went into the desert
and was tempted, perhaps himself trying out the total asceticism of John, the gospel says: "After John was put in
prison, Jesus went into Galilee, proclaiming the good news
of God. 'The time has come,' he said. 'The kingdom of God
is near. Repent and believe the good news!'" (1:14–15). Has
Jesus learned something in the desert about God that is good
news? In his A Life of Jesus, Shusaku Endo, the Japanese
novelist who is a Catholic, makes the following imaginative conjecture. In the desert Jesus learns that the seemingly
harsh and demanding God of John is really Abba, dear Father (or dear Mother since God has no gender), who wants
to be known as Love and who invites us all into the universal community of the Trinity.[3] We, too, in contemplation can
ask Jesus to reveal the deepest meaning of his message for us.

The next scene in the gospel is the peremptory call of the first four disciples. "As Jesus walked beside the Sea of Galilee, he saw Simon and his brother Andrew casting a net into the lake, for they were fishermen. 'Come, follow me,' Jesus said, 'and I will make you fishers of men.' At once they left their nets and followed him" (1:16–18). He does the same with the sons of Zebedee. What kind of man could so attract others? Do I want him to have that much power to attract me? Perhaps now I will find out how strong my desire to know and love and follow Jesus is.

When the disciples follow Jesus, what do they experience? The evil spirits recognize Jesus as their nemesis, and he casts them out with power. Moved with compassion he heals many people of their infirmities. One example is particularly revealing of who Jesus is. "A man with leprosy came to him and begged him on his knees, 'If you are willing, you can make me clean.' Filled with compassion, Jesus reached out his hand and touched the man. 'I am willing,' he said. 'Be clean!' Immediately the leprosy left him and he was cured" (1:40–42). Not only is Jesus compassionate enough to want to heal, but he goes further. In his compassion and love he touches this outcast, thus making himself ritually unclean and putting himself, according to the thought of the day, in danger of catching the disease. To grasp the enormity of his compassion we have only to think of the taboos and fears surrounding touching AIDS patients in our day when medical science knows so much more about how diseases are transmitted.

When Jesus touched the leper he was considered ritually unclean, but the gospel does not indicate that anything came of that. The very next healing, however, that of the paralytic brought in through the roof, begins a series of actions where Jesus gets into trouble with his own religious leaders. He forgives the sins of the paralytic. He eats with tax collectors and sinners. He does not follow the fasting ways of the

Pharisees or even of John. He cures on the Sabbath. This series of scenes ends with the ominous words, "Then the Pharisees went out and began to plot with the Herodians how they might kill Jesus" (3:6).

So the new disciples and we who ask to know Jesus in order to love him and follow him more closely experience a very complex man. He seems to know God intimately and so can act with compassion and healing even in defiance of customs and religious laws. He is not afraid of controversy. He draws great crowds not only because of his miracles, but also because of his message. He seems to bring out the fierce animosity and fear of the demons. Getting close to this man may be a dangerous thing. People who ask to know him better will experience both attractions and repulsions as they begin to realize the possible consequences of intimacy.

Before we look at the next scene, the call of the twelve apostles, let me underline the difference between who we are now as we ask to know Jesus better and who we *were* earlier when we desired to know that we were loved sinners. Earlier the focus was on ourselves and our need of forgiveness and assurance. We wanted to know that God was with us in our neediness and sinfulness. Some people, because of the hurts life has dealt them, never seem fully able to move beyond this point, and so can never fully desire to know Jesus in himself. For those who are able to move beyond this point, and it can only be done by the grace of God, the focus now is on Jesus. We want to know what he is like, what he values. And we want to be where he is. We may and will waver in this desire and shrink often from the consequences, but nonetheless our desire is to be with Jesus and our focus is on him.[4]

With these scenes as background we now come to contemplate the appointing of the twelve.

Jesus went up on a mountainside and called to him
those he wanted, and they came to him. He appointed
twelve — designating them apostles — that they might
be with him and that he might send them out to preach
and to have authority to drive out demons. These are
the twelve he appointed: Simon (to whom he gave the
name Peter); James son of Zebedee and his brother
John (to them he gave the name Boanerges, which
means Sons of Thunder); Andrew, Philip, Bartholomew,
Matthew, Thomas, James son of Alphaeus, Thaddaeus,
Simon the Zealot and Judas Iscariot, who betrayed him
(3:13–19).

As retreatants contemplate this scene, they have many reactions. Some stay on the edge of the crowd, timidly wondering
whether Jesus would want them to come closer. Others react angrily that there has to be a selection process at all, or,
as I indicated earlier, that Jesus only picks men as apostles.
Some are afraid that Jesus might notice them and ask them
to come forward. Some really want to be asked, but are afraid
that their hopes will be thwarted. Some notice the names
of the apostles and realize that one denied him three times,
none of them seemed to understand him during his lifetime,
one betrayed him for money, and all ran away in his time
of direst need. Close friends and companions of Jesus do not
have to be extraordinary or brave people at the beginning, it
seems. Some people feel more of a kinship with Jesus because
he, too, has been disappointed in at least one of his choices
of close friends. We might also notice that Jesus nicknamed
three of the apostles. Obviously, he was a creative and intu-
itive man. I wonder if the naming of the Sons of Thunder
showed his humor as well. Again all these reactions can enter into the dialogue with Jesus, but Ignatius would have the
retreatant look carefully at his or her desires during and after
this contemplation. What do I really want?

Before we leave the contemplation of this scene, let us
notice that Jesus calls the twelve "that they might be with

him and that he might send them out to preach and to have authority to drive out demons." Jesus wants and needs companions. Does he need them only for the mission, or does he need them also for himself? In other words, does Jesus desire them as friends as much as they desire him as a friend?

Many people have come to believe through their contemplation that Jesus desires their friendship and companionship even more than they desire his. And the desire is not utilitarian. That is, Jesus does not desire their friendship only because he needs workers in the vineyard. Jesus wants friends and companions. Just as he reveals himself to them, so too he wants them to reveal themselves to him. I underline this point because I know from personal experience that it is so hard for us to believe that Jesus really wants our friendship, a friendship that is mutual. "I no longer call you servants. . . . Instead, I have called you friends, for everything that I learned from my Father I have made known to you" (Jn 15:15).

Jesus, however, does also send the twelve out to preach and to drive out demons. He gives them the same mission that he has. Just as he came to call people to repent and believe the good news, so too these particular friends of his are called to do the same. Just as he came to oppose the powers of evil with his own power of love, so too these friends are sent to do the same. Obviously those chosen to be apostles are not super beings, but ordinary human beings with many flaws. For some reason, nonetheless, Jesus chose them, and one of them his betrayer, for the task of imitating him in the mission of wholehearted commitment to God's work of bringing about God's reign. There is a great mystery here, this matter of God's choice of individuals and even of a whole people for a particular task. This is the scandal of God's particularity.

That God has made such choices seems beyond doubt from the Bible. Examples are the choices of the Israelites as the Chosen People, of Moses, of Mary of Nazareth. What people have made of this choice has caused problems. Because of their choice as the Chosen People the Israelites seemed always prone to take pride in that choice, as though they deserved it. So, too, groups who believe that they have been chosen, as the apostles were chosen, to carry on in a special way the mission of Jesus have been prone to take pride in their position and to consider themselves on a higher plane in Christendom. Indeed, up until recent times the life of the vows of poverty, chastity, and obedience was considered a better way of life than marriage, and some religious gloried in that "superiority," even while mouthing the notion that they joined religious life to serve, not to be served.

The real question before a retreatant in the Spiritual Exercises at this point is this: Is God calling me to whole-hearted imitation of the poor Jesus? Will God allow me to follow Jesus in this way? The choice is up to God. Moreover, the choice does not, in my estimation, come down to a choice between being called to marriage or to religious life. People who are single, members of religious congregations, and the married can be called to radical discipleship. Some of the apostles in the New Testament, for example, were married, some apparently single. I have met people called to radical discipleship in all these walks of life.

Why some are called to such radical discipleship and others not is ultimately a question only God can answer. One answer may come from what I said earlier: Some people have been too hurt by life to be able to look very much beyond their own needs. I think, for example, of the man from whom a legion of demons was expelled. After the cure, "As Jesus was getting into the boat, the man who had been demon-possessed begged to go with him. Jesus did not let him, but said, 'Go home to your family and tell them how much the Lord has done for you, and how he has had mercy

on you'" (Mk 5:18–19). The man, apparently, did not bemoan this "rejection" as an injustice. Rather, "the man went
away and began to tell in the Decapolis how much Jesus had
done for him. And all the people were amazed" (20).

If one is called to radical discipleship, one ought to be
grateful rather than proud, grateful that one has whatever
qualities Jesus is looking for, grateful for the breaks of life
that make such a choice possible. I am reminded of J. D.
Salinger's story *Franny and Zooey*. Bessie, Franny and Zooey's
mother, has been pestering Zooey about his sister, Franny,
and has wondered about calling a psychoanalyst. In the
course of his response Zooey says,

> For a psychoanalyst to be any good with Franny at all,
> he'd have to be a pretty peculiar type. I don't know.
> He'd have to believe that it was through the grace of
> God that he'd been inspired to study psychoanalysis in
> the first place. He'd have to believe that it was through
> the grace of God that he wasn't run over by a goddam
> truck before he ever even got his license to practice.
> He'd have to believe that it's through the grace of God
> that he has the native intelligence to be able to help his
> goddam patients at *all*. I don't know any *good* analysts
> who think along those lines. But that's the only kind of
> psychoanalyst who might be able to do Franny any good
> at all.[5]

Jesus needs friends and disciples with that kind of gratitude
to God.

Questions for prayer and/or discussion:

1.   Do I have any desire to get to know Jesus better? Do I
want to desire a closer relationship with him? Can I tell him
what my real desires are?
2.   Can I believe that Jesus might want my friendship?

FOOTNOTES

1. *Autobiography, op. cit.*, p. 37.

2. Tetlow, *Choosing Christ in the World, op. cit.*, p. 149, italics mine.

3. Shusaku Endo, *A Life of Jesus*, Tr. Richard A. Schuchert (New York/Mahwah: Paulist Press, 1978).

4. This insight into the difference between the person of the First Week of the Exercises and the person of the Second Week I owe to William J. Connolly, S.J.

5. J. D. Salinger, *Franny and Zooey* (Toronto, New York: Bantam Books, 1964), p. 109.

CHAPTER 8

The Struggle Between
Jesus and Evil

In the previous chapter we noted the ferocity of the battle between Jesus and the demons in Mark's gospel. Our rationalistic age has difficulty believing in the existence of the devil. In fact, as a friend noted, serious talk about God has made a big comeback in recent years, but serious talk about the evil one is rarely heard, at least among the educated. Well, Ignatius of Loyola seriously believed in the existence of Satan and his helpers. Given the enormity of evil and hatred we have witnessed in this century, we might not be too far off in taking a leaf from his book.

On what Ignatius calls the fourth day of the Second Week of the Spiritual Exercises he asks retreatants to take time out from contemplating the public life of Jesus in order to reflect on the two value systems inculcated by Satan and by Jesus. Again Ignatius' military history comes out in the imagery he uses. Satan gathers his army under his standard or flag, and Jesus gathers his army under his standard. In the meditation on the "Two Standards," Ignatius' imagination rivals Cecil B. DeMille's: "Imagine you see the chief of all the enemy in the vast plain about Babylon, seated on a great throne of fire and smoke, his appearance inspiring horror and terror" (*Spiritual Exercises* n. 140). On the other hand, "consider Christ our Lord, standing in a lowly place in a great plain about the region of Jerusalem, his appearance beautiful and attractive" (*Spiritual Exercises* n. 144). Ignatius suggests that we try to imagine what a consummately evil person might look and feel like, and then try to imagine what Jesus might look and feel like.

Each of these adversaries has a program or system of values that he tries to inculcate in people. Last year during an undergraduate course in Ignatian spirituality I presented the program of Satan as Ignatius presents it. One of the students rather quickly asked whether I had seen the Woody Allen movie *Crimes and Misdemeanors*. I had not. She said that the movie pictured the value system of Satan. I was intrigued enough to see the movie, and sure enough, she was right.

The movie opens at a banquet honoring a very wealthy doctor for his philanthropy to a hospital. The doctor's wife and two children are there at the table with him basking in his reflected glory. But he has a problem that distracts him from the proceedings. His mistress is threatening to tell his wife all about their affair. It will, he believes, destroy his wife and ruin his own reputation. When his brother, who has mob connections, offers to have the mistress killed in such a way that no blame could attach to him, he is at first horrified, but eventually agrees that this is the only way out.

What has happened here? The doctor has wealth gained through his talent and training and work. This wealth enables him to live well, but also to give to worthy causes. He gains a reputation and honor in the community. His wealth also allows him to have a mistress whom he met on a business trip. Now, however, the mistress, who believed his story that he is sick of his wife and wants to marry her, stands in his way. Eventually, to save his reputation and honor he has his mistress' life snuffed out. He has arrogated to himself the right only God has. Pride led him to this horrible deed.

101

Here is how Ignatius describes the address of Satan to his minions.

> First they are to tempt people to covet riches (as Satan himself is accustomed to do in most cases) that they may the more easily attain the empty honors of this world, and then come to overweening pride.
> The first step, then, will be riches, the second honor, the third pride. From these three steps the evil one leads to all other vices (*Spiritual Exercises* n. 142).

Clearly the doctor in the film, who is not, by the way, a monster, has been seduced by this progression.

We need to look carefully at this process and notice how astute Ignatius is. Suppose a man has the brains and the opportunity to attain a doctorate. He is grateful to his family, his professors, his colleagues. With the doctorate he obtains a very good position at a prestigious university. He enjoys the prestige and the honor of being known as a member of this noted faculty. He wants to stay on this faculty, but to do that he needs to earn tenure. He is working on a research project that looks enormously promising, but one day he realizes that the numbers are not adding up the way he had predicted. He sees the research project going down the drain and tenure possibilities with it. He also sees that he could fudge the figures, and that no one would be the wiser. Has he succumbed to the pride that would say, "I deserve to be at this university. I've earned it"? If he has, then the temptation to falsify the data will be almost overwhelming.

This is the kind of progression Ignatius is describing. By riches Ignatius, it seems, means real wealth, but it does not have to be money, as in the example. Riches can be anything one acquires that brings one some honor or prestige. Then it is a relatively easy move to the belief that one deserves what one has and the honor and respect one receives. Pride is at one's elbow. That is why Zooey is right on the money when he says that the only psychoanalyst who could help his sister Franny is one who is grateful, one who is in reality humble.

The last remark leads us to the program Jesus recommends to all his helpers, as Ignatius articulates it:

> to seek to help all, first by attracting them to the highest spiritual poverty, and should it please the Divine Majesty, and should he deign to choose them for it, even to actual poverty. Secondly, they should lead them to a desire for insults and contempt, for from these springs humility.
>
> Hence, there will be three steps: the first, poverty as opposed to riches; the second, insults or contempt as opposed to the honor of this world; the third, humility as opposed to pride. From these three steps, let them lead people to all other virtues (*Spiritual Exercises* n. 146).

Spiritual poverty as something to be desired should pose no particular difficulty, even for the modern reader. Spiritual poverty means the same thing as Ignatius' "indifference," which Tetlow translates as "at balance." One so loves God that everything else is in proper perspective. It also means detachment as distinct from inordinate attachment or addiction as Gerald May uses these terms.[1] What this means is that we try to live in the real world in which all is gift. Nothing we have would be possible if we had not been created by God out of pure love and if we had not been helped along the way by myriads of people. Those who have the virtue of spiritual poverty are grateful people. Notice once again that Ignatius does not believe that anyone should choose actual poverty on his or her own. I may be attracted to living in actual poverty because I sense the real freedom such poverty would give me from the temptations of materialism or of power. But Ignatius suggests that I leave the choosing to God alone. I can ask to be chosen for the life of actual poverty, but I leave the actual choosing to God.

Insults and contempt are, perhaps, a different matter for us to understand. First, notice that Jesus wants people to

desire insults and contempt, not to bring them upon themselves. Second, desires are not under our control. If we do
not have the desire, the only thing we can do is to ask God
to give us the desire. Third, why might we desire insults
and contempt? Ignatius would answer that their opposite,
the honors of this world, are very dangerous, as we saw earlier when we reflected on the program of Satan. But then
Ignatius would add, "Jesus was treated with contempt and
insults, and those who love Jesus want to be like him in everything." Indeed, in the reflection he calls "Three Kinds of
Humility," he notes that the third

> consists in this. . . whenever the praise and glory of the
> Divine Majesty would be equally served, in order to imi-
> tate and be in reality more like Christ our Lord, I desire
> and choose poverty with Christ poor, rather than riches;
> insults with Christ loaded with them, rather than hon-
> ors; I desire to be accounted as worthless and a fool for
> Christ, rather than to be esteemed as wise and prudent
> in this world. So Christ was treated before me (*Spiritual
> Exercises* n. 167).

So the motive is love for Jesus. First and foremost, Ignatius
wants to be of service to God. Granted that primacy, then
Ignatius would want to be treated the way Jesus was treated
because he loves Jesus. The apostles after Pentecost provide
an example. When they had been flogged, they "left the
Sanhedrin, rejoicing because they had been counted worthy
of suffering disgrace for the Name" (Acts 5:41). Even here
we must note that the apostles do not choose the disgrace.
They receive it for proclaiming Jesus *and* they consider it a
great grace.

In the beginning of his conversion Ignatius let his fingernails and hair grow and in general looked and acted like
someone a bit crazy. This is how he interpreted the notion of
showing contempt for the ways of the world and of receiving
insults. Later, as he matured in his following of Christ, he

gave up these gestures because of his desire to be of service to others, but he still rejoiced when he suffered for preaching the gospel of Christ. Often enough novices in the following of Christ miss the point that Christ suffered insults and con-tempt not for dressing like a fool or a bum, but for speaking the truth.

In his inimitable style, Frederick Buechner takes off on gospel values:

> In the world of the fairy tale, the wicked sisters are dressed as if for a Palm Beach wedding, and in the world of the Gospel It is the killjoys, the phonies, the nit-pickers, the holier-than-thous, the loveless and cheerless and irrelevant who more often than not wear the fancy clothes and go riding around in sleek little European jobs marked Pharisee, Corps Diplomatique, Legislature, Clergy. It is the ravening wolves who wear sheep's cloth-ing. And the good ones, the potentially good anyway, the ones who stand a chance of being saved by God because they know they don't stand a chance of being saved by anybody else? They go around looking like the town whore, the village drunk, the crook from the IRS, because that is who they are. . . .
>
> And as for king of the kingdom himself, whoever would recognize him? He has no form or comeliness. . . . He smells of mortality. We have romanticized his rag-gedness so long that we can catch echoes only of the way it must have scandalized his time in the horrified question of the Baptist's disciples, "Are *you* he who is to come?" (Mt 11:13); in Pilate's "Are you the king of the Jews?" (Mt 27:11). . . . [2]

The potentially good, it should be noted, are those who recognize exactly who they are. They are, in other words, humble. Truth to tell, the wealthy and the powerful as well as the town whore and the village drunk are potentially good so long as they aspire after spiritual poverty. All that Jesus in the gospels and Ignatius in this meditation say is that riches

105

are a danger because they lead to honors and can lead a person to pride.

But we must not see this meditation as a cowboy movie where there are good guys and bad guys. True, the devil is consummately evil, and Jesus is good personified. But the battleground of these two ancient enemies is each human heart. None of us is immune to the blandishments of the evil one. Ignatius knows this truth with clarity. Indeed, all the saints have known, better than The Shadow of old radio days, "what evil lurks in the hearts of men." The closer they come to God, the more clearly they see how impossible it is for them to deserve this closeness, how sinful their hearts are.

Ignatius knows that the battleground is within each of our hearts, that each of us is very vulnerable to the siren call of Satan. Therefore he introduces for the second time in the Spiritual Exercises what is called the triple colloquy. The first time occurs when I want to know as fully as possible my sins and sinful tendencies and experience an abhorrence of them. In the present triple colloquy we are asked first to beg Mary, the mother of Jesus, to intercede for us with her son, then to beg Jesus to intercede for us with the Father, and finally to beg the Father for what we want.

We are asked first to address Mary,

> asking her to obtain for me from her Son and Lord the grace to be received under his standard, first in the highest spiritual poverty, and should the Divine Majesty be pleased thereby, and deign to choose and accept me, even in actual poverty; secondly, in bearing insults and wrongs, thereby to imitate him better, provided only I can suffer these without sin on the part of another, and without offense of the Divine Majesty. Then I will say the Hail Mary.

Because I know how vulnerable I am to the siren call, I need all the help I can get. Hence I ask Mary to intercede for me so that I may have the grace to embrace the values of Jesus.

After this first prayer I "ask her Son to obtain the same favors for me from the Father." Then I will say, "Soul of Christ," one of Ignatius' favorite prayers which he put at the head of the text of the Spiritual Exercises. Finally, with these two intercessors I "beg the Father to grant me the same graces. Then I will say the Our Father" (*Spiritual Exercises* n. 147).

Ignatius asks the retreatant to make this meditation four times in one day. That indicates how critical he believes it is that we know deep within us the attractions of both of these value systems in order to pray earnestly for the grace needed to live by the value system of Jesus.

Ignatius knows the matter of choice of a way of life is now at stake in the Exercises, so he proposes that the retreatant make a fifth meditation that same day on three classes of persons who have a choice to make. Each of these classes of persons has acquired by legitimate means a large sum of money, but they have not acquired it for the love of God. Each of them wants to do the right thing. They want to "find peace in God by ridding themselves of the burden arising from the attachment to the sum acquired, which impedes the attainment of this end," that is, peace in God (*Spiritual Exercises* n. 150). I imagine myself standing before God and all the saints and ask "for the grace to choose what is more for the glory of his Divine Majesty and the salvation of my soul" (*Spiritual Exercises* n. 152). Then he proposes how the three classes of persons deal with the problem.

The first class would like to do something. They may talk a great deal about what they should do, but they do nothing about it right up to the day of their deaths. The second class also wants to get rid of the attachment, but *they* decide how they will handle it. They will regularly give to the poor. The third class wants to get rid of the attachment, "but they wish

107

to do so in such a way that they desire neither to retain nor to relinquish the sum acquired. They seek only to will and not will as God our Lord inspires them, and as seems better for the service and praise of the Divine Majesty" (*Spiritual Exercises* n. 155). Many people are surprised at the way the third class handles the attachment; they expect that the best way would be to give away all the money. But that is not the wisdom of Ignatius. The third class wants to do their level best to find out what God wants them to do with the money. They want to let God decide for them. But Ignatius is astute enough to know how easy it is for us to rationalize our way to keeping the money. So he notes that

> when we feel an attachment opposed to actual poverty or a repugnance to it, when we are not indifferent to poverty and riches, it will be very helpful in order to overcome the inordinate attachment, even though corrupt nature rebel against it, to beg our Lord in colloquies to choose us to serve him in actual poverty. We should insist that we desire it, beg for it, plead for it, provided, of course, that it be for the service and praise of the Divine Goodness (*Spiritual Exercises* n. 157).

At the end of this meditation, once again the triple colloquy is made.

It may be appropriate at this juncture to note that Ignatius has a service mysticism. For whatever reason, his spirituality cannot rest in union with God or Jesus alone. Even though he loves Jesus with all his heart and wants to be treated the way Jesus was treated, he only wants this if it is for the service of God. As General of the Society of Jesus he will fight against every tendency among Jesuits to spend hours in prayer at the expense of apostolic service.[3]

We have here a very important point in Ignatian spirituality. Ignatius believes that God has hopes and dreams for each one of us and that God will make known his hopes and dreams in the concrete during these exercises (as well as at other times) if we give God a chance. Ignatius wants retreatants to open themselves to what God wants and then to beg for the grace to choose what God wants.

In Ignatian circles one often hears of the election that the retreatant must make during this period of the exercises. Usually people think that this election is the choice of the retreatant. Rather, we must think first that God is choosing or electing each one of us for some way of life that will be for our best interests and those of the community of all people in the Trinity. Only when we have discerned what God has chosen for us, do we have a choice of whether we will choose it or not. To make the choice along God's lines, Ignatius says over and over, we must beg God for the grace to do so. He knows how seductive is the siren call of the enemy of human nature.

Finally, I would suggest that in Mark's gospel we have two back-to-back scenes that illustrate very well the two value systems or standards we have been discussing.[4] In chapter six Herod gives a banquet for his own birthday, and Salome, his stepdaughter, dances and pleases the king. He promises to give her anything she wants, even half of his kingdom. Herodias, her mother, tells her to ask for the head of John the Baptist on a platter. Here we have the progression of Satan's standard acted out. Because of his wealth and position Herod has the honors of this world. Now faced with a moral dilemma, what does he do? "The king was greatly distressed, but because of his oaths and his dinner guests, he did not want to refuse her. So he immediately sent an executioner with orders to bring John's head" (Mk 6:26–27). Like the doctor in the movie *Crimes and Misdemeanors* he ends up taking a life to save face.

The very next scene in the gospel presents another banquet. When the disciples returned from their missionary journey, Jesus invited them on a vacation. The crowds got

109

wind of where they were going, however, and arrived before them. "When Jesus landed and saw a large crowd, he had compassion on them, because they were like sheep without a shepherd. So he began teaching them many things" (Mk 6:34).

Then came the question of how to feed the great crowd. The disciples wanted Jesus to send them away, but he answered, "You give them something to eat" (37). They had five loaves and two fish. "Taking the five loaves and the two fish and looking up to heaven, he gave thanks and broke the loaves. Then he gave them to his disciples to set before the people. He also divided the two fish among them all" (41). However we interpret this miracle, we see in it Jesus' and the disciples' poverty. Not only do they not have the means to feed the people, but they also have to forego their vacation. However, we also see a willingness to share whatever little they had with others. Moreover, Jesus lets the apostles pass out the bread and fish. One can interpret this gesture as Jesus' willingness to share the admiration of the crowd with them.

Jesus faces us squarely with the choice of serving God or money (Lk 16:13). On this day of the Spiritual Exercises Ignatius faces the retreatant with the same choice. It is the age-old choice put so well in Deuteronomy.

> See, I set before you today life and prosperity, death and destruction. For I command you today to love the Lord your God, to walk in his ways, and to keep his commands, decrees and laws; then you will live and increase. . . .
>
> Now choose life, so that you and your children may live and that you may love the Lord your God, listen to his voice, and hold fast to him (Deut 30:15–20).

It is no more easy for us to choose life than it was for the Israelites. That is why Ignatius continually exhorts us to beg for the grace to be put under the standard of Christ.

Questions for prayer and/or discussion:

1. Do I see in my own life how the value systems of Satan and of Christ operate?
2. Can I see these value systems operative in the social structures of my city, country, church? How do I react?

FOOTNOTES

1. Gerald G. May, Addiction and Grace (San Francisco: Harper & Row, 1988).

2. Frederick Buechner, Telling the Truth: The Gospel as Tragedy, Comedy and Fairy Tale (New York: Harper & Row, 1977), pp. 89–90.

3. See Harvey D. Egan, Ignatius Loyola the Mystic (Wilmington, DE: Michael Glazier, 1987) where all the dimensions of Ignatius' own mystical experiences and their implications for Ignatian spirituality are comprehensively treated.

4. For this suggestion I am again indebted to William J. Connolly.

CHAPTER 9

Discipleship:
Shaping a Life

The whole section of Mark's gospel beginning at 8:22 and ending at the end of chapter 10 is bound together by the story at the beginning and the story at the end. Each is a story about the cure of a blind man. The first cure, you may recall, was a gradual one. Jesus touched the blind man's eyes with spittle and the man saw people, but like trees walking. After the second touch he saw clearly, and Jesus sent him home (Mk 8:22–26).

At the end of chapter 10 we read about the cure of the blind beggar Bartimaeus, who was cured by a word from Jesus and who "followed Jesus along the road" (Mk 10:46–52). In between these two cures Jesus predicts his passion three times, and three times the apostles miss the point; they are blind. In this section Jesus seems to be teaching them what discipleship means.

It is significant, I believe, that the first blind man is sent home after the cure, while Bartimaeus follows Jesus on the road, or, in other translations, on the way. Jesus is about to go on the way of the cross. The early Christians were called "people of the way." Thus, Bartimaeus can be seen as a type of disciple who has been healed of blindness and sinfulness and who now follows Jesus on his way, which is the way of the cross.

Immediately after the cure of the first blind man Jesus asked the disciples, "Who do people say I am?" They replied, "Some say John the Baptist; others say Elijah; and still others, one of the prophets." "But what about you?" Jesus asked, "Who do you say I am?" Peter answered, "You are the Christ," that is the Messiah or Anointed One (Mk 8:27–29). In the context of the gospel Peter's recognition of Jesus' identity seems to lead Jesus to begin to reveal more and more of himself and of what being the Christ would mean.

> He then began to teach them that the Son of Man must suffer many things and be rejected by the elders, chief priests and teachers of the law, and that he must be killed and after three days rise again. He spoke plainly about this, and Peter took him aside and began to rebuke him.
>
> But when Jesus turned and looked at his disciples, he rebuked Peter. "Out of my sight, Satan!" he said. "You do not have in mind the things of God, but the things of men" (Mk 8:31–33).

In the synoptic gospels (Matthew, Mark, and Luke) the confession of Peter at Caesarea Philippi seems to be the point of no return for Jesus. From this point on the die is cast. Three times he predicts his coming passion. Taking the gospel as the story it is, one can almost sense Jesus' urgency to have the disciples understand what kind of Messiah he is — indeed, who God really is. If Jesus, the Messiah, will give up his life out of love, then God is not the God who devours his enemies but a God who is self-sacrificing love.

Clearly, Peter did not understand. Who can blame him? Even after almost two thousand years of reading and hearing the gospel and of reflecting on it, most of us, most of the time, do not, in our heart of hearts, really believe that this is who God is. Would we be so afraid of God's vengeful wrath if we believed this about God? Would so many people for so

113

many years have believed that missing Mass on Sunday was a sin meriting hell? or eating meat on Friday? Would we so easily call down God's wrath on our enemies? Would we vote for the death penalty?

Deep within many of us sits an image of God as one who does exact an eye for an eye. So we give lip service to the idea that Jesus, the Messiah, is a suffering servant, but it does not much impinge on our lived lives. More power to Peter, then, that he could say out loud what most of us would have felt in our hearts. "No way! When the Messiah comes, we will be vindicated; we will triumph. None of this stuff about suffering and crucifixion!"

But Jesus comes right back at Peter, at the one who is to be the leader of this group of disciples, and in front of the rest rebukes him. "You do not understand God at all!" If we think that this is a just world where the good always win and are rewarded in this life, then not only do we not understand the world, but we do not understand God. Jesus knows that he will not win by the standards most people set for being successful.

Jesus also understands the God he calls "Abba," dear Father. God really does want human beings to enter into community with God and one another, and God will not let even our hatred and the murder of God's beloved Jesus change who God is. We can refuse God's offer, ultimately and willfully. God will not coerce us into community. If God did coerce us, we would not form a community, but a benevolent dictatorship. God wants friends, not slaves. If God will not coerce us, however, then we can turn our backs on God's offer. Jesus sees the storm clouds of fear and envy and hatred looming toward him. He intuits that he will not win in the way the disciples expect him to win. He will, nonetheless, continue to carry on God's ways, preaching the good news of the reign of God, even in the face of impending suffering and death. God does not change, no matter what we do to thwart God's intention. Indeed, whatever hell is, it is not God's vengeance. The suffering Messiah guarantees this truth. At the heart of Jesus' teaching about who he is and what discipleship means is the identity of God. God is self-sacrificing love. There is no way around this fact if Jesus is the final revelation of God.[1]

For the moment I will pass over the very next passage in which Jesus talks about the consequences for those who follow after him. I want to continue the teaching about who the Messiah is. Chapter 9 begins with the transfiguration of Jesus before Peter, James, and John on the mountain. Some scholars have referred to this scene as a post-resurrection scene brought into the public life. I see no reason not to take it on its own terms as something that happened to Jesus in an ecstatic moment. In the history of spirituality saints have been described as somehow transfigured by an ecstatic experience of God. Why not Jesus? The disciples see Jesus transformed before their eyes, and then "a cloud appeared and enveloped them, and a voice came from the cloud: 'This is my Son, whom I love. Listen to him!'" (9:7).

The scene reminds us of the baptism of Jesus when the same voice spoke to him as "my Son, whom I love." The disciples are to listen to him. What does Jesus tell them? "As they were coming down the mountain, Jesus gave them orders not to tell anyone what they had seen until the Son of Man had risen from the dead. They kept the matter to themselves, discussing what 'rising from the dead' meant" (9:9). Again Jesus speaks of his death and resurrection, but though they are puzzled about "rising from the dead," they do not pursue this matter further with Jesus, perhaps again because they cannot fathom the concept of "losing" in this way.

Later in chapter 9 this scene occurs.

> They left that place and passed through Galilee. Jesus did not want anyone to know where they were, because

115

he was teaching his disciples. He said to them, "The Son of Man is going to be betrayed into the hands of men. They will kill him, and after three days he will rise." But they did not understand what he meant and were afraid to ask him about it (9:30–32).

Jesus, it seems, is painstakingly trying to get across to them the real situation of his and their mission. Again fear keeps them from inquiring further. They go on to prove in action that they still have not understood, for the gospel continues: "They came to Capernaum. When he was in the house, he asked them, 'What were you arguing about on the road?' But they kept quiet because on the way they had argued about who was the greatest" (9:33–34). How dense can they be? Jesus once again tells them that he is the suffering servant, and they argue about who is number one! So Jesus tries again. "Sitting down, Jesus called the Twelve and said, 'If anyone wants to be first, he must be the very last, and the servant of all'" (9:35). Then Jesus returns to the idea that misunderstanding who he is means to misunderstand who God is. Conversely, if we understand who Jesus is and imitate him as a servant of all, we understand God and imitate God and welcome God.

The third prediction of the passion indicates how ominous the situation had become. Listen to the tone of the opening words.

> They were on their way up to Jerusalem, with Jesus leading the way, and the disciples were astonished, while those who followed were afraid. Again he took the Twelve aside and told them what was going to happen to him. "We are going up to Jerusalem," he said, "and the Son of Man will be betrayed to the chief priests and teachers of the law. They will condemn him to death and will hand him over to the Gentiles, who will mock him and spit on him, flog him and kill him. Three days later he will rise" (10:32–34).

Some people who have contemplated this scene after the other two prediction scenes have had the impression that Jesus might have needed and wanted companions who could really be with him in this dark hour, could really understand him and be for him. If that was the case, he was once again disappointed as we hear in the next section. James and John came to Jesus and asked him if they could sit at his right and his left in his glory. Once again we see how their values differed from those of Jesus and how blind they were to what he was trying to teach them. Then when the other ten heard about their request, they became indignant with James and John. So Jesus patiently tried once again to communicate his value system.

> "You know that those who are regarded as rulers of the Gentiles lord it over them, and their high officials exercise authority over them. Not so with you. Instead, whoever wants to become great among you must be your servant, and whoever wants to be first must be slave of all. For even the Son of Man did not come to be served, but to serve, and to give his life as a ransom for many" (10:42–45).

Perhaps now we can see why this section is bounded by the cures of blind men. The disciples are certainly blind. And Jesus could not be clearer about his own identity and, therefore, God's identity and about what discipleship would mean. In this last passage, by the way, we can see echoes of the two standards that Ignatius puts before retreatants just before they begin to reflect on their own way of life. The standard of Satan progresses from riches to honor to pride; the standard of Christ from poverty to insults to humility.

Let us now return to the section after the first prediction of the passion. Jesus has just rebuked Peter.

> Then he called the crowd to him along with his disciples and said: "If anyone would come after me, he must deny himself and take up his cross and follow me.

117

For whoever wants to save his life will lose it, but whoever loses his life for me and for the gospel will save it.
What good is it for a [person] to gain the whole world,
yet forfeit [one's] soul? Or what can a [person] give in
exchange for [one's] soul? If anyone is ashamed of me
and my words in this adulterous and sinful generation,
the Son of Man will be ashamed of [that person] when
he comes in his Father's glory with the holy angels" (Mk
8:34–38).

To come after Jesus means to be a disciple, to imitate Jesus
in his passionate commitment to the reign of God — to be
with him about his Father's business. Such following means
trying to live out God's intention for the universe and for me
in such a way that nothing else matters as much. Even life
itself is not a good to be clung to if attachment to it gets in
the way of living out God's intention. We are reminded here
of Ignatius' principle of indifference toward — "at a balance
before" (in Tetlow's translation) — all created persons and
things. That compares with God's desire in creating us and
our own deepest desire to be one with God, Father, Son, and
Holy Spirit in their one action which is the universe.

But, of course, no one is, or even can be, indifferent or
at balance without the grace of God. We are all too attached
to the things of this world, to our reputations, to our goods,
to our pleasures, to our very lives. Gerald May maintains that
we are all addicted to something that keeps us from fully desiring what we most deeply want, namely God. Moreover,
our efforts to save ourselves from our addictions only dig us
deeper into the hole. Only God's grace can save us from our
addictions.[2] Once again we note the wisdom of Ignatius in
the meditation on the two standards. He knows that the battleground is within our hearts and that we are helpless before
the siren call of our attachments without the grace of God.
Hence he insists that we must beg Mary to intercede for us
to obtain the grace to have our hearts accept the standard
or value system of Christ, to beg Christ himself to intercede

118

with his Father for the same grace, and to beg the Father also. We cannot do it by ourselves.

Before we leave this section on discipleship, I want to say something about the two motives, love and fear. John Macmurray notes that love and fear are the primary human motives. Love is care and concern for the other(s); fear is fear for oneself. What all human beings want is to live without fear. In my terms, we want what God wants for us; namely, to live in a community where fear is subordinated to love. When I am afraid, I pull back from love for others; in effect, I abandon community in order to protect myself. I may band together with some people like myself to protect myself and us from the "outsiders," but neither my group nor I really have what we most deeply want because we fear the outsiders who could take away what we are protecting.

In the passage cited from Mark about denying self Jesus is speaking to this very dilemma, I believe. In order to have life we must not be afraid to lose it. If we try to protect ourselves from any loss because of fear, we are trapped. We cannot enjoy that which we are protecting. But we are bedevilled by fears, are we not? — fears about our health, our reputation, our security, our future, our very life. May would say that we are addicted to these things. Ignatius, in the Principle and Foundation, counsels us to be indifferent to or at balance toward them. But, we have already noted, before addictions we are helpless.

Where Ignatius and May urge us to beg for God's grace, Macmurray takes a more philosophical tone, as one would expect from a philosopher. He states that religion is the only solution for the dilemma of being human, but it must be real religion. He makes this trenchant comment on the difference between real and illusory religion.

> All religion . . . is concerned to overcome fear. We can distinguish real religion from unreal by contrasting their

119

formulae for dealing with negative motivation. The maxim of illusory religion runs: "Fear not; trust in God and he will see that none of the things you fear will happen to you"; that of real religion, on the contrary, is "Fear not; the things that you are afraid of are quite likely to happen to you, but they are nothing to be afraid of."[3]

Paul knew well the struggle between his deepest desires and the other siren calls of his heart. This passage from the Letter to the Romans sums up well the last points we have been discussing.

So I find this law at work: When I want to do good, evil is right there with me. For in my inner being I delight in God's law; but I see another law at work in the members of my body, waging war against the law of my mind and making me a prisoner of the law of sin at work within my members. What a wretched man I am! Who will rescue me from this body of death? Thanks be to God — through Jesus Christ our Lord! (Rom 7:21–25).

Questions for prayer and/or discussion:

1. What are my reactions as I read this chapter? Can I tell Jesus these reactions?

2. How much of my life is controlled by the motive of fear? Do I want to live with less fear? Can I ask Jesus for help to become more like him?

FOOTNOTES

1. See John E. Smith, *Experience and God* (New York: Oxford, 1968), p. 80.

2. May, *Addiction and Grace, op. cit.*

3. John Macmurray, *Persons in Relation* (London: Faber & Faber, 1961), p. 171.

CHAPTER 10

Sharing the Passion and Resurrection of Jesus

No matter how close two friends or lovers are, at some point in the relationship one of them will fall gravely ill and eventually die. The closer two people are the more painful the suffering and separation is for both of them. Neither wants the other to suffer and to leave. If my friend suffers, I suffer; if he or she dies, part of me also dies. We are persons precisely because of our relationships. Without some you, to whom I am related personally, I am nothing.[1] A friend is *dimidium animae meae*, half of my soul, as the Roman poet Horace says and Augustine repeats.

Because the suffering and death of someone close is so painful, loneliness is part of the process. My friend who is suffering and dying does not want to add to my grief, so she does not tell me what she is going through. I do not want to add to her sufferings, so I do not tell her how I am feeling. Moreover, I do not know whether dwelling on her pain and fears of death will make matters worse. Thus I do not ask her to tell me what she is experiencing. In addition, since I may not want to face the fact that my friend is dying, I may presume that she does not want to face it either. It could even be that I am angry that my friend is leaving me, even angry at her. My friend could be angry at me because I will go on living. There are many dynamics that keep us from sharing with very close friends the suffering and dying all of us must face.[2]

What a great gift it would be if friends could share together these moments just as they have shared so much in their lives! It might make the time even more painful, but it would relieve the loneliness and allow them to stay as intimate as possible even to the last. It may break my heart to experience such a friendship, yet my tears of sorrow would mix with tears of joy that not even suffering and death had been able to keep two friends from intimate conversation right to the end.

In our previous chapter we followed Jesus' public life to the point in Mark's gospel where Bartimaeus, cured of his blindness, "followed Jesus along the road" (Mk 10:52). We noted that the "road" is the road to Calvary since the very next lines in chapter 11 describe the triumphal entry into Jerusalem which ushers in the last week of Jesus' life. The Spiritual Exercises presume that retreatants who have grown to know and love Jesus deeply in order to follow him more closely will desire to share his passion. This desire ushers in what Ignatius calls the Third Week. Ignatius puts the desire this way, "to ask for sorrow, compassion, and shame because the Lord is going to his suffering for my sins" (*Spiritual Exercises* n. 193).

Two points need to be emphasized, I believe. First, as we noted earlier, our desires, and especially the deepest desires of our hearts, are not in our control. We cannot make ourselves desire union with God, intimacy with Jesus, or to share Jesus' passion. Ignatius expects that God will elicit the desires that are most for our good if we open ourselves and our hearts to God's tutelage and if we ask God to give us these desires. Thus, if we do come to desire to share Christ's passion, to have sorrow and compassion for him, that desire is God's doing, not ours. Hence, if we have this desire, God must want us to have it, and for our good. But perhaps God wants us to have it also for Jesus' sake. Perhaps Jesus wants us to share in his passion and death as part of our mutual friendship. It is possible, in other words, that it is a comfort to Jesus that people continue to want to share with him his experience of the passion. Now that is a mind-boggling thought, isn't it?

Second, we can think that having compassion for Jesus will be easy now that we have come this far in our friendship with him. But that is not so, just as it may not be easy to have compassion for a very close friend who is suffering and dying. Ignatius is, once again, an astute spiritual director. We desire and ask for sorrow and compassion; we ask for a grace that is not in our power to produce in ourselves. Indeed, if you have ever experienced real sorrow and compassion for a loved one who was suffering and dying, did you not feel that this compassion was a gift? Your friend trusted you with what he or she was undergoing. Perhaps it was also a gift of God that you were not so absorbed in your own grief that you could be present to your friend. So we are asking for the gift, the grace of sorrow and compassion for Jesus.

The experience of this part of the Spiritual Exercises differs widely depending on the retreatants' past experiences with suffering and death. Some people get very angry at God at some time during this period of the Spiritual Exercises, angry that God lets the son he called his beloved die so horribly, just as God let some loved one die horribly. Others get angry at all the horrors God allows to happen in this world as images are brought to mind by the contemplation of the passion of Christ — images of torture of the innocent, of concentration camps and gas chambers, of abused and battered and starving children. Others focus on every figure in the story of the passion except Jesus. They become angry at the apostles, look down on people like Judas, Herod, and Pilate, and see the crowds as just as fickle as any crowd can be. They unconsciously resist focusing on Jesus because his pain is too much to bear or, perhaps, because his passion and death remind them of their own mortality.

Some people even get angry at Jesus because it looks almost as though he is bringing this fate upon himself. Some are puzzled that they seem to feel nothing as they try to contemplate the passion. The grace of compassion does not come easily to us because of these and other such reactions. If any one incident in the history of the world blows away the just world hypothesis by which most of us unconsciously live, it is the cruel suffering and death of the sinless one. Contemplation of his passion faces us with what we fear the most, death and its capriciousness and its often enough terrible companion, severe suffering.

No matter what our reactions, we need to continue the practice inculcated earlier in the Exercises of letting God and Jesus know them. If we find that the desire to know Jesus' experience of the passion has waned or even disappeared because of these reactions, we can, if we want, ask that the desire return in vigor. If we still feel the desire in spite of our resistances, we can continue to beg for the grace of sorrow and compassion for Jesus. Again there is no time limit by which the grace must be attained. Many people have made the thirty-day retreat and not yet received this grace at the end. It may take years to attain a really deep sorrow and compassion for Jesus. In fact, most of us probably go through cycles of deepening compassion for Jesus throughout our lifetimes. After all, the liturgical cycle brings us face to face with the passion of Jesus each year. One of the functions of this yearly return may be to allow us to enter ever more deeply into his sorrow and suffering.

People do receive the gift of sorrow and compassion for Jesus, and they know that their sorrow is different from what they experienced in the First Week of the Exercises when they contemplated Jesus on the cross. Then they were sorry for their sins and marveled at Jesus on the cross, who still looked on them with love in spite of the sins which had put him there. Now they do not focus on themselves much at all, but on Jesus and what he has gone through and is going through. One woman came in during a retreat with tears streaming down her face and said, "He's dead; I'm glad that his agony is over." And people who receive this grace of compassion for Jesus find that the compassion spills over to compassion for all the suffering people of this world. Indeed, they sense that Jesus is still suffering in all the people who suffer, especially in those who are oppressed and ground down as he was. I think that such compassion for a suffering world means taking on the heart of Christ and the compassion of God. God, I believe, is revealing his own reactions to the horrors human beings perpetrate on one another and on God's beloved Jesus. The mystical body of Christ is experienced in a mysterious way when God gives us this gift of compassion for Jesus' suffering and the suffering of untold others.

Christians believe that Jesus was raised from the dead, but have we ever experienced what that means for Jesus and for our world? In the Spiritual Exercises Ignatius expects that those who have received, in some measure, the grace of compassion for Jesus and his sufferings, both personal and in his mystical body, will begin to desire to experience the joy of Jesus' resurrection. Once again, under the tutelage of the Holy Spirit of God, retreatants are expected to desire "the grace to be glad and rejoice intensely because of the great joy and the glory of Christ our Lord" (*Spiritual Exercises* n. 221). We notice once again that we are desirous of a grace, not something in our power to achieve. Note also that we want to rejoice for Jesus' sake.

The fact that we are asking for a grace should alert us to the possibility that the grace may not be easily attained, not because God withholds it, but because we seem to resist it. This seems paradoxical. One would think that we would be

125

eager to attain this grace after suffering with Jesus through the passion. But look at the stories of the resurrection appearances in the gospels. The usual pattern runs like this. Something happens that seems to raise hopes, the tomb is empty, a stranger appears and sets the disciples' hearts burning, angels tell them that he is risen, and they are afraid yet filled with joy. But they do not recognize the stranger, or they are afraid or bewildered. Finally they come to the recognition that it really is Jesus, and they are overcome with joy and belief. What makes it so hard for the friends of Jesus to receive the grace of joy in his resurrection?

Let's look carefully at one of these appearances, the appearance on the road to Emmaus (Lk 24:13–32). You recall the story. Two disciples started on the road to Emmaus even though they had heard reports that the women found the tomb empty. On the road they met a stranger. When they told the stranger the events of the past few days concerning Jesus of Nazareth, the stranger said to them,

> "How foolish you are, and how slow of heart to believe all that the prophets have spoken! Did not the Christ have to suffer these things and then enter his glory?" And beginning with Moses and all the Prophets, he explained to them what was said in all the Scriptures concerning himself (25–27).

Later we hear that their hearts were burning within them as they walked with this stranger and he talked, but they still did not recognize him nor did they pay attention to their hearts. They did not want to let him go, however, and prevailed on him to stay with them for a meal during which they recognized him in the breaking of the bread.

I believe that this story gives us a clue as to why the grace of the joy of the resurrection is resisted. The resurrection is not a restoration of the *status quo ante*, of things as they were before the passion and death. It does not erase those cruel memories. No! The Christ had to die in this

way in order to be who he now is. In other appearances this
"necessity" is underscored by the fact that the disciples see
the marks of the nails and of the wound in his side. The
past with all its cruelties is not undone. In fact, without
that past Jesus would be different from the person he now
is. But the disciples and we, too, want the cruel memories to
be erased. "It was only a bad dream," we hope to be able to
say. We do not want to face the truth that only through the
actual life and death he and we undergo can we attain the
joy of resurrection.

This resistance sits deep within all of us. We do not want
to face the fact that we can have life and really enjoy it only
if we accept death and all that death represents. Erikson
maintains that the final developmental stage in life brings
on the crisis between ego integrity or wisdom and despair. He
defines wisdom as "the acceptance of one's one and only life
cycle as something that had to be and that, by necessity, admitted of no exceptions."[3] Such wisdom, he maintains, leads
to freedom from the inordinate fear of death. If God and I do
accept me as I now am, then we accept everything that has
happened to make me who I am. It could have been different, but this is the way my life was. This is the meaning of
Erikson's "something that had to be and that, by necessity,
admitted of no exceptions." This is, I believe, the meaning of
Jesus' words in the Emmaus story, "Did not the Christ *have to*
suffer these things and then enter his glory?" The wisdom of
Jesus accepts what has happened as the only way he could be
who he now is.

It is very hard for us to come to this wisdom. In fact,
on our own we cannot. We need the grace of God. Hence,
we must beg God to be able to rejoice with Jesus. To rejoice
with him we must accept his cruel death. It was not a bad
dream. Just as the pains and sufferings and losses we suffer
and will suffer in life are not bad dreams. I believe that we
also cannot fully rejoice in the life of our loved ones who

have died and experience their risen life until we can accept their suffering and death. Not only does the fear of death keep us from fully enjoying this life, it also keeps us from rejoicing with the risen Jesus and with our loved ones who have joined him.

I want to repeat once again Macmurray's maxim of real religion. "Fear not; the things that you are afraid of are quite likely to happen to you, but they are nothing to be afraid of."4 The resurrection of Jesus demonstrates real religion. The passion and death really did happen, but, the resurrection of Jesus says, they are nothing to be afraid of. When we receive the grace of rejoicing with Jesus in his glory, then we want to shout Alleluia over and over again.

For me the scene in literature that comes closest to expressing the feelings one experiences with this grace comes in the last volume of Tolkien's great trilogy, *The Lord of the Rings*. The Dark Lord has been vanquished and the world saved. Frodo, the Hobbit or Halfling, had carried the Ring of Power to the edge of the Crack of Doom with great heroism and self-sacrifice. At the end he could not bring himself to throw the ring into the Crack of Doom and thus save the world. A crazed figure, Smeagol, whom Frodo had spared earlier in the drama, appears suddenly, struggles with Frodo, bites off Frodo's ring finger, and in his triumph at finally getting back the ring falls into the Crack of Doom. The world is saved this time by an act of mercy, namely Frodo's act, which preserved the life of the crazed Smeagol. Now Frodo and his faithful servant Sam are recovering from their wounds and do not yet know that the world has been saved. Gandalf, the wizard and their great friend whom they thought dead, wakes Sam. Sam wakes from sleep, smells beautiful perfumes, sees Gandalf, and says:

> "Gandalf! I thought you were dead! But then I thought I was dead myself. Is everything sad going to come untrue? What's happened to the world?" "A great Shadow has

departed," said Gandalf, and then he laughed, and the
sound was like music, or like water in a parched land;
and as he listened the thought came to Sam that he
had not heard laughter, the pure sound of merriment,
for days upon days without count. It fell upon his ears
like the echo of all the joys he had ever known. But he
himself burst into tears. Then, as a sweet rain will pass
down a wind of spring and the sun will shine out the
clearer, his tears ceased, and his laughter welled up, and
laughing he sprang from his bed.

"How do I feel?" he cried. "Well, I don't know how
to say it. I feel, I feel" — he waved his arms in the air
— "I feel like spring after winter, and sun on the leaves;
and like trumpets and harps and all the songs I have
ever heard!"[5]

A short while later Frodo and Sam are led before all the
armies who have been fighting against the Dark Lord, and as
they approached, "swords were unsheathed, and spears were
shaken, and horns and trumpets sang, and men cried with
many voices and in many tongues.

"Long live the Halflings! Praise them with great
    praise!
Praise them with great praise, Frodo and Samwise!
Praise them!
Praise them!
Praise them! The Ring-bearers, praise them with
    great praise!"[6]

This scene comes as close as anything I've ever read in
literature to expressing our feelings about Jesus at Easter.
Moreover Frodo and Sam realize that they have not wak-
ened from a bad dream because Frodo has no ring finger, just
as Jesus has the wounds of his passion.

Questions for prayer and/or discussion:

1.   Have I experienced the difficulty of sharing a loved one's
pain?

2. Have I experienced the presence of Jesus risen or of a loved one who has died?
3. What gives me my greatest happiness?

FOOTNOTES

1. This notion of the person as being constituted by relationships has been developed best, to my knowledge, by John Macmurray in *Persons in Relation* (London: Faber & Faber, 1961).

2. For some of the dynamics of dying see Elisabeth Kübler-Ross, *On Death and Dying* (New York: Macmillan, 1969).

3. Erik K. Erikson, *Childhood and Society*, 2nd ed. (New York: Norton, 1963), p. 268.

4. Macmurray, *op. cit.*

5. J. R. R. Tolkien, *The Return of the King* (Boston: Houghton Mifflin), p. 230.

6. *Ibid.*, p. 231.

CHAPTER 11

Finding God in All Things

W e come to the end of this journey with God, Father, Son, and Holy Spirit under the tutelage of Ignatius' Spiritual Exercises. After the Fourth Week, Ignatius adds a *"Contemplatio ad amorem,"* which is generally translated as "Contemplation to Attain the Love of God." Tetlow paraphrases it, "The Contemplation for Learning to Love Like God."[1] Before he presents the exercise Ignatius makes two points.

1. The first is that love ought to manifest itself in deeds rather than in words.

2. The second is that love consists in a mutual sharing of goods, for example, the lover gives and shares with the beloved what he possesses, or something of that which he has or is able to give; and vice versa, the beloved shares with the lover.
Hence, if one has knowledge, he shares it with the one who does not possess it; and so also if one has honors, or riches. Thus, one always gives to the other (*Spiritual Exercises* nn. 230–231).

The first point is obvious even if difficult to put into practice. The second point bears some reflection.

Love is described as a mutual sharing of what one has and is. Thus, God, who is love, shares with us what he has and is. We would not exist if God did not share life with us

131

out of love. Moreover, as we have often said in this book, God shares with us not just physical life on this planet, a gift enough, but wants to share with us God's own community life. God is continually creating this universe with the one intention of inviting all persons into the community life of the Trinity.

The even more mind-boggling corollary of the point about mutuality of sharing is that God desires that we share what we have and are with God. Through his experience Ignatius came to believe that God wants our love, wants a mutual friendship. Moreover, as we have repeatedly noted, the community to which we are called is one where everyone always gives to the other or others. The community each of us has with the Trinity includes in principle everyone who is invited into that community. It is a universal community. If I could always give to the other, that would mean that I was not worried about myself, was not protective of myself. Perfect love would have cast out fear (see 1 Jn 4:18). John Macmurray says that what we all desire at our deepest level is community whose ideal "is a universal community of persons in which each cares for all the others and no one cares for himself."[2] Ignatius' formulation of the second point mentioned above at least moves in the same direction, only he comes to his notion from his own mystical experience and his own philosophical and theological studies.

The mention of Ignatius' mystical experience leads to a comment about the exercise Ignatius puts at the end of his Spiritual Exercises. Ignatius calls it a contemplation, not a meditation. In a meditation we reflect on the mystery with which we are presented. In a contemplation we hope that we will experience God's own presence. It is well to remember this distinction when we come to the exercise proper. Ignatius asks us to desire "an intimate knowledge of the many blessings received, that filled with gratitude for all, I may in all things love and serve the Divine Majesty"

132

(*Spiritual Exercises* n. 233). When, in the contemplations on the public life of Jesus, I desired "an intimate knowledge of our Lord, who has become human for me, that I may love him more and follow him more closely," I was asking for a personal revelation of Jesus to me. So, now, I am asking for a personal revelation of the many blessings God has given me. Ignatius does not believe that he was singled out for the revelations he had because of any merit of his; everything he received he thought of as a gift. Hence he expects that anyone can ask God for such a revelation and then hope that God will respond.

In his *Autobiography* Ignatius recounts a few of the experiences he had at Manresa that seem to be the background for his points in the "Contemplation to Obtain Love." First, after noting that he had a great devotion to the Holy Trinity, but little understanding of the theological reflection on this mystery, he tells about this experience.

> One day while saying the Hours of Our Lady on the steps of the monastery itself, his understanding began to be elevated so that he saw the Most Holy Trinity in the form of three keys. This brought on so many tears and so much sobbing that he could not control himself. . . . As a result the impression of experiencing great devotion while praying to the Most Holy Trinity has remained with him throughout his life.

In a footnote the editor of my edition of the *Autobiography* notes that "(t)his image or figure of the Trinity refers to the keys — *teclas* — of a musical instrument and probably signifies a musical chord — three notes producing a single harmony."[3]

Ignatius continues to a second illumination.

> One time the manner in which God had created the world was revealed to his understanding with great spiritual joy. He seemed to see something white, from which some rays were coming, and God made light from this. But he did not know how to explain these things, nor

did he remember very well the spiritual enlightenment
that God was impressing on his soul at that time.[4]

Note the vagueness of this illumination. Often we think
of the "illuminations" and "revelations" of saints as though
they were pictures on a canvas. Perhaps we have intimations
of such "illuminations" in our own experience, but we do
not give them credence. Do you sometimes sense the whole
world as somehow or other tied together and held in love?
Here are a couple of examples from citizens of Britain who
responded to a request from a researcher for instances of religious experience.

> I heard nothing, yet it was as if I were *surrounded by
> golden light* and as if I only had to reach out my hand to
> touch God himself who was so surrounding me with his
> compassion.[5]

> It seemed to me that, in some way, I was extending into
> my surroundings and was becoming one with them. At
> the same time I felt a sense of lightness, exhilaration,
> and power as if I was beginning to understand the true
> meaning of the whole universe.[6]

> One night I suddenly had an experience as if I was
> buoyed up by waves of utterly sustaining power and
> love. The only words that came near to describing it
> were "underneath are the everlasting arms," though this
> sounds like a picture, and my experience was not a pic-
> ture but a feeling, and there were the arms. This I am
> sure has affected my life as it has made me know the
> love and sustaining power of God. *It came from outside
> and unasked.*[7]

The people who described these experiences were just
ordinary folks like us. So perhaps Ignatius is not too far off
the mark when he advises retreatants to voice the desire for
an intimate knowledge of the blessings received from God.
Ignatius, by the way, begins the list of experiences of illumination he had at Manresa in the same paragraph that begins,
"God treated him at this time just as a schoolmaster treats

a child whom he is teaching." In other words, these experiences occurred when he was still young in the spiritual life. Here is how he describes the third experience.

> One day in this town while he was hearing Mass in the church of the monastery mentioned above, at the elevation of the Body of the Lord, he saw with interior eyes something like white rays coming from above. Although he cannot explain this very well after so long a time, nevertheless what he saw clearly with his understanding was how Jesus Christ our Lord was there in that most holy sacrament.[8]

Once again notice that the vision is interior and that it is more than just visual. His understanding is involved. Perhaps we have such intuitions about the presence of the Lord in the eucharist.

The fact that Ignatius' "visions" contain very little of visual content shows itself even more clearly in the next experience he narrates.

> Often and for a long time, while at prayer, he saw with interior eyes the humanity of Christ. The form that appeared to him was like a white body, neither very large nor very small, but he did not see the members distinctly. He saw this at Manresa many times. . . . The things he saw strengthened him then and always gave him such strength in his faith that he often thought to himself: if there were no scriptures to teach us these matters of the faith, he would be resolved to die for them, only because of what he had seen.[9]

Whenever I read these lines, I feel consoled because I have no idea of how to describe the Jesus I contemplate, yet I, too, believe that I have encountered him and gained some interior knowledge of him.

The fifth experience is the vision on the banks of the river Cardoner near Manresa.

> While he was seated there, the eyes of his understanding began to be opened; though he did not see any vision,

135

he understood and knew many things, both spiritual
things and matters of faith and of learning, and this was
with so great an enlightenment that everything seemed
new to him. Though there were many, he cannot set
forth the details that he understood then, except that
he experienced a great clarity in his understanding. This
was such that in the whole course of his life, through
sixty-two years, even if he gathered up all the many
helps he had had from God and all the many things he
knew and added them together, he does not think they
would amount to as much as he had received at that
one time.[10]

These, then, are the experiences of contemplation that
are generally considered the sources of the points Ignatius
asks the retreatant to ponder in the contemplation to obtain
love. The desire, again, is that God will give an intimate
knowledge of God's many blessings. Let us go through the
four points of this exercise.

The first point "is to recall to mind the blessings of creation and redemption, and the special favors I have received"
(Spiritual Exercises n. 234). In a sense we return here to the
Principle and Foundation, only now with all the experiences
of the Exercises as further background. Ignatius says:

I will ponder with great affection how much God our
Lord has done for me, and how much he has given me
of what he possesses, and finally, how much, as far as he
can, the same Lord desires to give himself to me according to his divine decrees.[11]

Let your mind and heart be filled with the memories and the
present realities that God has done and is doing for you out
of love. God does not just give gifts, God gives God's own
self. Do you sense almost a poignancy in the words, "how
much, as far as he can, the same Lord desires to give himself to me"? God wants to give more and more of God's self
but cannot, both because of our resistance and also because
of our finite limitations. But, one gets the impression from

Ignatius' words, how God yearns to give us even more, wants us to share all the joy of the inner life of the Trinity!

If we were to experience even in a little way how much God gives of God's own life and yearns to give even more, then we would want to give what we have and are to God in mutuality. Remember Ignatius' words about love showing itself in mutual sharing. What do we have to give to God? Ignatius says, "all I possess and myself with it." He then proposes that I make this offering:

> Take, Lord, and receive all my liberty, my memory, my understanding, and my entire will, all that I have and possess. You have given all to me. To you, O Lord, I return it. All is yours, dispose of it wholly according to your will. Give me your love and your grace, for this is sufficient for me.[12]

I have come to believe that all that I have and am includes not only the faculties Ignatius mentions, but all my reactions as well. Mutuality means that I want to let God know my loves and my hates, my joys and my sorrows, my lusts, my addictions, my weaknesses and my strengths. In my last retreat I sensed that Jesus wanted me to give him all that goes on in my heart, that he really meant it when he called his disciples friends, and that he calls me friend. Friends show their love by revealing themselves without fear, even when what is revealed seems unsavory. Jesus reveals himself without fear to us, and he wants us to reciprocate. Moreover, he seems grateful when we do. When and insofar as we deeply appreciate how much God shares and wants to share of God's own self with us, then we spontaneously want to give all of ourselves. It is difficult for us to believe, however, (at least, it is difficult for me to believe) that God really wants us to share all our reactions with him. But I believe that it is true.

In the second section of the contemplation Ignatius invites me

137

> to reflect how God dwells in creatures: in the elements
> giving them existence, in the plants giving them life, in
> the animals conferring upon them sensation, in human
> beings bestowing understanding. So he dwells in me and
> gives me being, life, sensation, intelligence; and makes
> a temple of me, since I am created in the likeness and
> image of the Divine Majesty (*Spiritual Exercises* n. 235).

I am then invited to reflect on myself as in the first point
or in some other way that may seem better. Here we are
asking to experience how holy the universe is, how sacred.
We want to experience this, not just conclude to it from
theological premises. Of course, we do, at times, have such
experiences, fleeting moments when we sense the sacredness
of everything. But what we want is such a deep experience
that it will affect how we act in this world. To be a con-
templative in action is to contemplate (or find) God in
our daily lives, in our activity. If we were contemplatives in
action, we would approach everyone and everything with
reverence. One of my friends tries to thank the vegetables
and the animals that have provided the meal we are about
to have. I believe that Ignatius is speaking of this kind of
reverence.

Here is Ignatius' third point.

> This is to consider how God works and labors for me in
> all creatures upon the face of the earth, that is, he con-
> ducts himself as one who labors. Thus, in the heavens,
> the elements, the plants, the fruits, the cattle, etc., he
> gives being, conserves them, confers life and sensation,
> etc.
>
> Then I will reflect on myself (*Spiritual Exercises*
> n. 236).

You can see how the Principle and Foundation of the beginning of the Exercises is recapitulated in this contemplation.
All the creatures on the face of the earth are there to help us
to attain our end of divine union. I would ask you to recall
how Ignatius, in the First Week, reflected with astonishment

that all creatures had continued to sustain and help him even though he was such a sinner. Now we ask to experience how God acts as a laborer to create the whole universe for the sake of the community of all persons with the Trinity.

In the fourth point Ignatius seems to be trying to describe some of the illuminations mentioned earlier.

> This is to consider all blessings and gifts as descending from above. Thus, my limited power comes from the supreme and infinite power above, and so, too, justice, goodness, mercy, etc., descend from above as the rays of light descend from the sun, and as the waters flow from their fountains, etc. (*Spiritual Exercises* n. 237).

If we could only experience all blessings and gifts as descending to us from above, then we would be able to live in spiritual poverty. We would be "indifferent to," "at balance toward," all created gifts and blessings because we would have intimate knowledge that these are only pale, even though wonderful, reflections of the deepest desire of our hearts, God, "from whom all blessings flow." To God, Father, Son, and Holy Spirit be honor and glory and praise forever and ever. Amen.

Questions for prayer and/or discussion:

1. Have I had any experiences of God's creative presence in my life? How did I feel?
2. Would I want to be more aware of God's presence in my everyday life? What might keep me from desiring an awareness of God's presence?

FOOTNOTES

1. Tetlow, *Choosing Christ in the World*, op. cit., p. 172.
2. Macmurray, op. cit., p. 159.

3. *Autobiography, op. cit.*, pp. 37–38.

4. *Ibid.*, p. 38.

5. Alister Hardy, *The Spiritual Nature of Man: A Study of Contemporary Religious Experience* (Oxford: Clarendon Press, 1979), p. 20.

6. *Ibid.*, p. 21.

7. *Ibid.*, pp. 76–77.

8. *Autobiography, op. cit.*, p. 38.

9. *Ibid.*, pp. 38–39.

10. *Ibid.*, pp. 39–40.

11. *Ibid.*

12. *Ibid.*